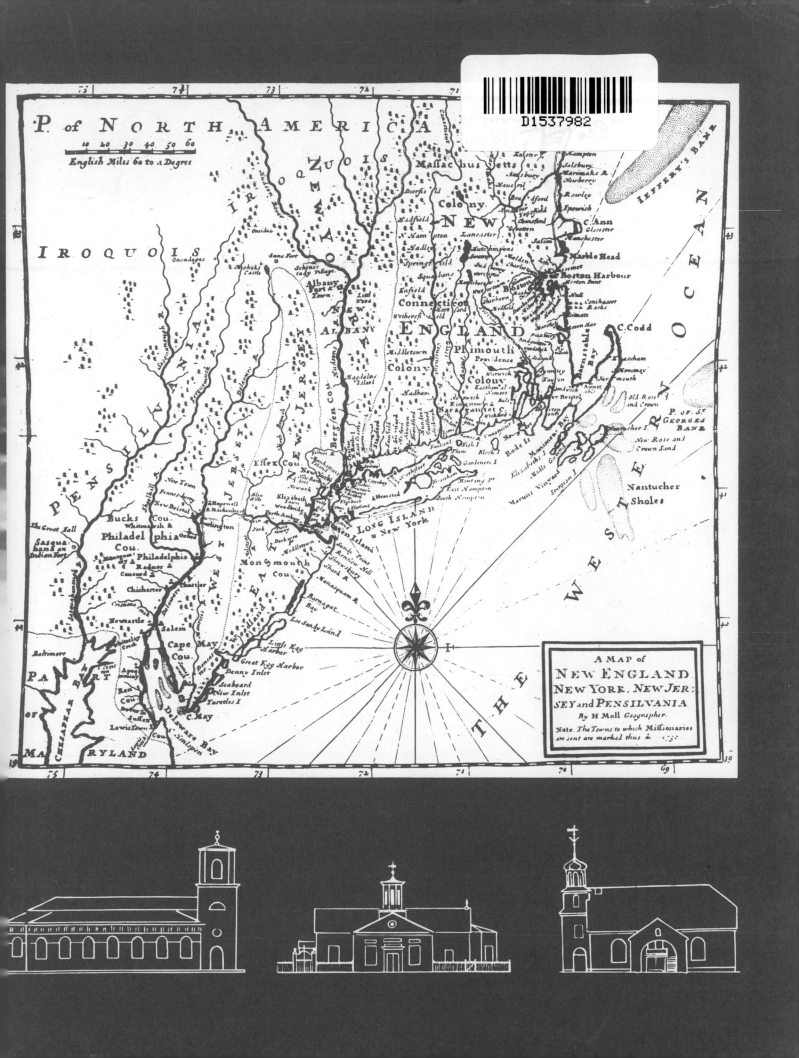

A MAP of
NEW ENGLAND
NEW YORK, NEW JER:
SEY and PENSILVANIA
By H Moll Geographer.
Note. The Towns to which Missionaries
are sent are marked thus

1607

EARLY ENGLISH CHURCHES IN AMERICA

1807

1. *Bruton Parish Church, Williamsburg, Virginia,* 1711

EARLY ENGLISH

CHURCHES IN AMERICA

1607-1807

STEPHEN P. DORSEY

New York · OXFORD UNIVERSITY PRESS · 1952

Copyright 1952 by Oxford University Press, Inc.

LIBRARY OF CONGRESS CATALOGUE CARD NUMBER: 52-9429

PRINTED IN THE UNITED STATES OF AMERICA

To

THE MEMORY OF MY MOTHER

Julia Geisthardt Dorsey

PREFACE

THE FOLLOWING PAGES form a visual essay primarily addressed to those who are interested in American architecture and history. Without attempting to be a comprehensive architectural analysis or to give a complete historical account of each building, the book aims to portray the rich heritage of English colonial design, craftsmanship, and history in a group of old churches.

The book is confined to the early Episcopal churches in the United States, which were built during the first two centuries after the Church of England was successfully planted on the western shores of the Atlantic in 1607. These early churches, which still exist in numbers along the eastern seaboard of the United States from New Hampshire to South Carolina, lend themselves to special study apart from the contemporary buildings of other Churches. In contrast to the others, during most of the period they were united by a common responsibility to the same ecclesiastical authority in England, by their use of the liturgy of the Book of Common Prayer, and by many traditional practices which, even in a reformed setting, most of the exclusively Protestant groups rejected as smacking of 'popery.' As a result the 'English Church,' as it was known in many colonial communities, had certain physical characteristics, particularly with regard to its interior furniture, that set it apart from the meeting-houses and chapels of the 'dissenting' bodies. Moreover, in a number of the original thirteen colonies, as in England, the Anglican Church was the established or state church. It continued, after its disestablishment as a purely English institution, to be one of the strongest ties between Americans and the other English-speaking peoples.

The author's purpose is threefold—to arouse general interest in the restoration of some of these old buildings to their original beauty and in the preservation of other more remote examples now in danger of destruction through decay; to increase the understanding of those who are interested in the early history of the Protestant Episcopal Church or indeed of the United States; and, by an examination of this facet of our many-sided common heritage, to strengthen further the bond between Americans and their British cousins.

The introductory chapter outlines the historical background of the Protestant Episcopal Church and its beginnings in the United States. The second chapter describes the distinctive features that characterized the setting of Anglican worship in America during the seventeenth and eighteenth centuries, and points out the influences and laws that governed the setting. Subsequent material summarizes the history of the Church and the architecture of its buildings in each major region of the eastern coast: Virginia and Maryland, the Carolinas, the Middle States, and New England, from the beginnings of the various colonies through the year 1807.

The structures illustrated were selected to depict general regional characteristics as well as the several types of church buildings in each region. Where numerous examples were available, those buildings, or parts of buildings, are presented which are the finest architecturally, or possess the greatest historical interest, and which today are unaltered or in certain respects most resemble their original appearance. Inevitably it has seemed necessary to place somewhat greater emphasis on those areas in which the greatest number of early churches are found today. The lists of church buildings appended to these chapters, to the best of the author's knowledge, include all the churches of the Anglican Communion built before 1808 that are still standing and are not in a ruined state, even though their appearance may now be greatly altered. There may be omissions of buildings located in less traveled places, but these are not intentional. Compilation of the lists has involved not only correlation of a vast amount of written material from various sources, but the searching of records, checking with diocesan authorities, and personal visits.

As shown by the illustrations, these old churches are of various architectural types. While a great many are essentially unchanged or have been restored to their original appearance, too many others still suffer from our grandfathers' unfortunate adventures in medievalism of the William Morris variety. When obtainable, the date of the beginning of each structure has been used rather than that of its completion. Owing to the scarcity of funds and materials, the period of construction of a church in the seventeenth and eighteenth centuries was frequently of some years' duration. Moreover, this procedure seems consistent with the fact that in most colonial vestry books orders for the construction of new churches or accounts of the laying of foundation stones figure more prominently than notices of completion of the edifices. The latter date received less emphasis, as the buildings were often used for some time in a semi-finished state, particularly in rural areas. The period covered ends approximately with the first decade of the nineteenth century.

To many, the timbers, brick, and stone of the houses in which men have worshiped for generations take on a special beauty that is not given to places devoted to the more ordinary aspects of human existence. It is hoped that the beauty of these old buildings will provide new interest and inspiration to those who take the author's pilgrimage.

ACKNOWLEDGMENTS

THE AUTHOR ACKNOWLEDGES his grateful appreciation to the Bishops, Historiographers, and other diocesan officers for their general interest and information regarding the lists of churches; to the Reverend John Wallace Suter, D.D., formerly Dean of Washington Cathedral, and the Reverend George J. Cleaveland, Canon Librarian of Washington Cathedral, for their continued interest and most helpful criticism; to the Reverend Frederic S. Fleming, D.D., and the Reverend Robert C. Hunsicker of the Parish of Trinity Church in the City of New York; the Reverend George MacLaren Brydon, D.D., Historiographer of the Diocese of Virginia; George Carrington Mason, formerly Historiographer of the Diocese of Southern Virginia; and George W. Williams of St. Michael's Church, Charleston, South Carolina, for review of certain portions of the manuscript; to the rectors and parishes furnishing photographs and information; to Carolyn C. Dorsey and Guy P. Dorsey for their unfailing encouragement and assistance in the preparation of the manuscript and photographs; to Mathilde D. Williams of the Peabody Library of Georgetown, D.C., for assistance in research; and to Elizabeth T. Sprague, Pauline E. Huntemann, and Helen Brice for preparing the material for publication.

Many of the photographs in the book have been drawn from the files of the Historic American Buildings Survey Collection in the Library of Congress, an invaluable asset to any student of American architectural history. In large part these photographs are the work of Frances Benjamin Johnston, Francis Marion Wigmore, John O. Brostrup, C. O. Green, and the late Thomas Tileston Waterman. Virginia Daiker of the Library of Congress has been tireless in the aid she has given the author in using the facilities of the Survey.

Special assistance in securing other photographic material has been generously given by: Helene Owen of the Parish of Trinity Church in the City of New York; Dorothy C. Barck of the New-York Historical Society; the Reverend F. H. Craighill of Bruton Parish Church, Williamsburg, Virginia; Marian Osborne of Colonial Williamsburg, Williamsburg, Virginia; the Reverend Allen Evans, D.D., of St. Peter's Church in the City of Philadelphia; the Reverend John P. Mitton of Caroline Church, Setauket, New York; the Reverend Robert H. Dunn of St. John's Church, Portsmouth, New Hampshire; the Reverend Alex C. D. Noe of St. Thomas' Church, Bath, North Carolina; the

Reverend John H. Thomas of All Saints' Parish, Leonardtown, Maryland; the Reverend Palfrey Perkins, D.D., and Priscilla Darling of King's Chapel, Boston; Samuel Chamberlain of Marblehead, Massachusetts; Francis C. Lincoln of New York; Mrs. Philip B. Wallace of Philadelphia; Harold S. Davis, Bradford Eddy, and Asa E. Phillips, Jr., of Boston; Mary Ronald Bent and Halsted B. Vander Poel of Washington, D.C.; Richard M. Coit of New Canaan, Connecticut; C. W. Kellogg of Queen Anne, Maryland, and many others.

CONTENTS

PLATES

I

Historical Background

ESTABLISHMENT OF THE CHURCH OF ENGLAND IN AMERICA

WHEN WE FIRST WENT TO VIRGINIA,' wrote Captain John Smith, in *Advertisements for the Unexperienced Planters of New England*, 'I well remember, wee did hang an awning (which is an old saile) to three or four trees to shadow us from the Sunne, our walles were rales of wood, our seats unhewed trees, till we cut plankes; our Pulpit a bar of wood nailed to two neighboring trees; in foul weather we shifted into an old rotten tent, for we had few better, and this came by the way of adventure for new. This was our Church, till wee built a homely thing like a barne, set upon cratchets, covered with rafts, sedge, and earth; so was also the walls; the best of our houses of the like curiosity, but the most part farre much worse workmanship, that could neither well defend wind nor raine, yet wee had daily Common Prayer morning and evening, every Sunday two sermons, and every three moneths the holy Communion, till our Minister died. But our Prayers daily, with an Homily on Sundaies, we continued two or three yeares after, till more Preachers came.'[1]

Thus the Church of England was successfully established on the western shores of the Atlantic in the spring of 1607, only fifty-eight years after the first compiling of the Book of Common Prayer and four years before the King James version of the Bible was published. On 29 April the colonists had set up a cross at the point of their first landing at Cape Henry and here beneath the 'old saile' was held a celebration of the Holy Communion on the Third Tuesday after Trinity, 21 June 1607.

English Christianity had already briefly touched the continent of North America in several places. As early as 24 March 1498, an entry in the privy-purse accounts of Henry VII reads, 'to Lanslot Thirlkill, of London, upon a prest for his shipp going towards the New Islande, £20.'[2] It was not until 1578, however, that the services of the Book of Common Prayer of the reformed Church of England are known to have been read on North American soil. In July of that year, Maister Wolfall, priest of the Church of England and chaplain of the fleet under command of Martin Frobisher, celebrated the Holy Communion according to the 1559 Book of Common Prayer on the shores of Frobisher Bay. In the following year the Reverend Francis Fletcher, chaplain of Drake's ship, *Pelican*, first held services from the Prayer Book on the shore of San Francisco Bay. Of Raleigh's ill-fated colony, established by Sir Richard Grenville on Roanoke Island in 1585, we know that the Reverend Thomas Hariot baptized the first white English child, Virginia Dare, in 1587. And in Whitsuntide, 1605, prayers, probably from the Prayer Book of 1604, were used by members of George Waymouth's expedition at the erection of a cross on Monhegan Island off the coast of Maine.

The colony of Virginia was not entirely an imperialistic and commercial venture. The third name on the list of patentees is that of the Reverend Richard Hakluyt, Prebendary of Westminster and the great chronicler of English voyages, who became titular rector of Jamestown—Robert Hunt accompanying the first settlers as his vicar. The third article of the King's Letters Patent commends the desire to further the propagation of the Christian religion, and in the Articles, Instructions, and Orders to the colonists, it is provided that the president, Council, and ministers 'with all diligence, care and respect doe provide that the true word, and service of God and Christian faith be preached, planted, and used, not only within every of the said several colonies, and plantations, but alsoe as much as they may amongst the salvage people which doe or shall adjoine unto them, or border upon them, according to the doctrine, rights, and religion now professed and established within our realme of England.'3

The men who brought the Church to the new world were products of the political and religious conflict and of the vigorous, striving, glorious Elizabethan era—an age of incredible personal courage, audacious exploration, and brilliant learning. They were only a generation removed from the break with Rome under Henry VIII and the fury of the struggle between zealots of both the extreme Protestant and Catholic parties under the boy King Edward and his sister Mary, who succeeded him. Many of them had witnessed Elizabeth's controversy with both groups of extremists, and their spiritual food had been the third Prayer Book of 1559, which was characteristic of her statesmanship. The Prayer Book of 1559 had been drafted to make it acceptable to the bishops who had been exiled under 'Bloody Mary' and, at the same time to free it of any taint of heresy from a biblical, patristic, conciliar Catholic point of view.

LAUDIAN RECONSTRUCTION AND PURITAN REACTION

Only three years before the establishment of the Church in Virginia had occurred the coronation of James I—an event which was followed by almost four decades of reconstruction and consolidation of the Church of England. At the Hampton Court Conference in 1604 the King effectively supported the Church against all attempts to change its nature. In the following years Richard Hooker vindicated its doctrine, and the saintly Launcelot Andrewes, Bishop of Winchester, upheld its historical position.

Not only in his writings, but in his life, Andrewes was a strong link between the old and the new in the Church of England. In spite of the unpopularity of the practices he advocated, such was his greatness that he was able to pursue his life serenely, virtually without attack. Content to enforce on others a minimum standard of formality in the conduct of public worship, Andrewes maintained his right to set an example for them by exercising in his own chapel the full ancient ceremonial of the church—with cope, lights, and incense.

It was not so with William Laud, the other great supporter of the Church, who was raised to the Primacy eight years after Charles I ascended the throne in 1625. His ardent devotion to his church coupled with a highly dictatorial nature obscured his greatness as a theologian and a patron of learning and identified him with a system opposed to the traditional political liberties of Englishmen. Like Andrewes, he sensed the significance and greatness of the English Church whose position was both Catholic and anti-papal, and whose appeal was both scriptural and historical. Unfortunately, his methods were not so wise as his concepts. Despite his hostility to papal doctrine and his equal opposition to Calvinism, his support of an increasingly distasteful royal government kindled a popular hatred that eventually brought him to the block.

When he became Archbishop of Canterbury, the same energy which, as Bishop of London, he had devoted to the reform of Oxford University, to the restoration of old St. Paul's, and to work in the Privy Council, was turned to stamping out all signs of Puritan nonconformity. The communion tables were railed in and set back altar-wise against the east walls of the churches. Parishioners were required to make their communion three times yearly, to kneel at its reception, to uncover their heads during the services, and to bow at the name of Jesus. They were commanded to attend their own parish churches, where use of the surplice was enforced. Children and servants were required to be catechized, and Sunday gambling, drinking, and trading was forbidden. Rich and powerful offenders were punished as well as those who were poor. A commission of which Laud was a member had been given authority over administration of the colonial Church in 1634, and parsons abroad in the colonies were required to subscribe to the Act of Uniformity and the use of the whole services prescribed in the Prayer Book and none other.

Good as his intentions were, Laud's system brought not only the opposition of the Puritans, who connected it with Roman beliefs, but of the man in the street, whose indifference it reprimanded and whose pleasures and vices it restrained. Moreover, its rigorous reform offered no real solution to England's religious complications and failed to recognize the fact that Puritanism had become one of the lasting factors in English religious life.

William Laud fell with King Charles. When the Long Parliament took the affairs of the nation into its hands, the Archbishop was accused of high treason by the House of Commons and was removed to the Tower. He was not tried until three years later, and although his defense was able, his doom was a foregone conclusion, and he was beheaded in January 1644.

Meanwhile twelve of the bishops were sent to prison. Episcopacy and the Book of Common Prayer were abolished, and seven thousand of the clergy were turned out of their livings and forbidden to preach or administer the sacraments. Not only was an assembly established to draw up a new book of public worship, a new catechism, and a different form of church government, but the Commons appointed a committee to oversee the destruction of stained glass and carved stonework as monuments of superstition. It was a return to the fanatical destruction of Christian art that had characterized the reign of Edward VI. As Lord Protector, Cromwell, who favored independency, saw to it that in Puritan England a man was free to profess any faith so long as it was not Anglican, Roman Catholic, or Unitarian.[4]

In New England the revolution brought widespread rejoicing. In Virginia, where there had been a strong tinge of Puritanism in local churchmanship, but where there was also very real enthusiasm for the Stuart kings and the established Church, Charles II was immediately proclaimed King after the execution of his father.[5] However, the colony could not hold out alone against the Commonwealth, and under the terms of submission it was agreed that the Book of Common Prayer might continue to be used for one year, provided public prayers for the king were omitted from the liturgy. It seems probable, however, that during the period of Puritan rule the services were carried on with very few changes, although there was some decay of the colonial Church owing to its inability to secure additional badly needed ministers and a not unnatural public reluctance to show any too obvious opposition to the Commonwealth government.[6]

THE RESTORATION

With the restoration of Charles II to the throne in 1660, the Church of England came back to its own both at home and in the colonies. By act of Parliament the ousted clergy were restored, and the property confiscated during the civil war was returned to the Church. In March 1661 the Savoy Conference was called, with twelve bishops and twelve Puritan members summoned to see whether an adjustment of their differences might not be made. When it became clear that their positions were irreconcilable, the Conference came to an end and the convocation turned to the problem of revising the Prayer Book. The book issued in 1662, which has become such an integral part of the English tradition, was a revision of the 1559 version improved from a liturgical and devotional point of view to bring it closer to the ancient traditions of the Church.

The flight from England of the avowed Romanist, James II, after a brief reign of three years, and the accession of William of Orange and Mary, James' daughter, as joint sovereigns in 1688 came at a time when the national Church was becoming rather clearly divided into two distinct schools of religious thought and political inclination. One group, standing for a Laudian return to the historical traditions of the Church and to her discipline, identified themselves closely during the reign of Charles II with the Tory doctrine of hereditary right in the Crown. The other group, the Low Churchmen or Latitudinarians, as strongly opposing the religious enthusiasm of the High Church traditionalists as they did that of the dissenting Baptists and Quakers, emphasized the importance of reason and a sort of decorous restraint in religious matters. Forming a distinct school of their own within the Church, they made up a strong wing of the Whig party, which supported the political principle of the magisterial view of kingship as opposed to the High Church and Tory concept of hereditary right.

With the transfer of the crown to William, unfortunately not only some distinguished laymen, but the Archbishop of Canterbury, five bishops, and four hundred parish clergy persisted in the view that they could not take an oath to a new sovereign unless they were released by James from the allegiance they had sworn to him. The clergy were of course deprived of their charges. Bishop Ken, who gave us the Doxology, was one of this number.

These Non-Jurors, who left their posts for conscience's sake, are of special interest because as Free Evangelical Catholic churchmen, bound neither by convocation nor Parliament, they were able to revive the ancient liturgy of the Church without let or hindrance. When Samuel Seabury secured his consecration at the hands of the Scottish successors of these Non-Jurors, he promised to introduce the ancient liturgy of St. James into the American Prayer Book. The result was the superb Prayer of Consecration in the Communion Service familiar to all members of the Episcopal Church in this country.

One must also question what stronger effect upon the development of the Church of England in America might have resulted during the colonial period had the Non-Jurors not been driven from the official organization of the Church of the eighteenth century. Certainly the commissary system provided an inadequate substitute for the American episcopacy, which was desired by many American churchmen and which was repeatedly refused by the Whig party. Backed by a number of the clergy and influential laymen of Pennsylvania, New Jersey, and Maryland, who complained that 'Our Churches remain unconsecrated, our children are grown up and cannot be confirmed,' the Reverend John Talbot of Burlington, New Jersey, for almost two decades pleaded with the authorities in London to send a suffragan bishop to America. His second mission to England in 1720 for this purpose was unsuccessful. We know now that on that trip he was irregularly consecrated in the non-juring succession in the summer of 1722, along with Dr. Richard Welton, briefly rector of Christ Church, Philadelphia, from 1724 to 1726.[7]

THE SOCIETY FOR THE PROPAGATION OF THE GOSPEL

The end of the seventeenth century marked a turning point in the life of the Church of England as far as the colonies overseas were concerned. In 1699 the Reverend Thomas Bray, who had been appointed as Commissary of the Bishop of London in Maryland, founded the Society for the Promotion of Christian Knowledge. The first meeting took up three major subjects: the support of religious education in primary schools, the support of the Church in the colonies, and the circulation of Christian literature at a minimum cost to the reader.[8] In 1701, through Bray's efforts, the Society sponsored the founding of a new project, The Society for the Propagation of the Gospel in Foreign Parts, for the express purpose of supporting the work of the Church of England in the colonies. Its charter provided that both Archbishops, the Bishops of London and Ely, the Deans of Westminster and St. Paul's, the Archdeacon of London, and the Regius and Lady Margaret Professors of Divinity of Oxford and Cambridge Universities should always be members of the Society.[9] Thus the Archbishops, the Diocese of London, and the Universities were united in support of this tangible recognition of the Church's duty to minister to the colonies.

The seal of the Venerable Society, as it has come to be known, may be seen in plate 2. It depicts 'A ship under sail, making towards a point of Land, upon the Prow standing a Minister with an open Bible in his hand, People standing on the shore in a Posture of Expectation and using these words: Transiens Adjuva Nos ("Come over and help us").'[10] The Society's missionary did not come unless a request had been received from the community, which made some provision for his needs. The Society for the Propagation of the Gospel made up the balance required for his support from funds collected from donors throughout England. During the years from 1702 to 1783 no less than 353 S.P.G. missionaries were sent to the American colonies. Their semi-annual reports, plus the numerous letters interpreting colonial society and customs they sent home to the London office, numbering over 50,000 manuscript pages, form probably the greatest single existing archive of exact information on eighteenth-century life in the English colonies in America.[11]

In a pioneer land where one of the greatest hungers was for the literature of the mother country, a chest of books was given to each outgoing clergyman for his own use and to serve as a lending library for his parishioners. Not only did the Society contribute

1500 volumes to King's College (now Columbia University), which was founded largely under Anglican sponsorship, but it made several sizable gifts of books to both Yale and Harvard, over neither of which it had control or influence.[12]

The maps at the beginning and end of the book, which were published in London in 1730, show that by that date the Society's missionaries were serving churches from South Carolina to Massachusetts. The Venerable Society's policy was a wise one. As soon as the community that had asked for aid could take over support of the parish, the S.P.G. withdrew to new missionary fields.

The foundation of the Society for the Propagation of the Gospel in Foreign Parts was a logical offspring of the deep religious enthusiasm that characterized the reign of Queen Anne. Innumerable early American parishes pride themselves on the communion vessels marked with the royal cipher, which were sent to them during this period. It was likewise a great period of building among colonial American churches as is indicated in the following pages. The Church in America owes an incalculable debt to the S.P.G., without which it probably would never have become more than a weak Church restricted to a narrow section of the country.

INFLUENCE OF THE WHIGS ON THE AMERICAN CHURCH

The accession of George I in 1714 brought an end to the vigorous growth of the Church in England that had marked the reign of Queen Anne. The Whig party, representing the great landowners and merchants, was able to prevent any Tory from being called into the king's inner counsels from that date until 1761. In its support of the Hanoverian succession and its fear of the Jacobite inclinations and High Church zeal of the country squires and clergy, who were strong elements in the Tory party, the Whig government made equally certain that, as new bishops were appointed, they reflected the political inclinations and religious Latitudinarianism of the party in power. For the same reasons the convocations, or periodic deliberative and legislative assemblies of the Church, which, except during the Commonwealth, had met regularly for eleven centuries, were suppressed not to meet again until 1850.[13]

Deistic philosophy certainly did much to dull the spiritual sensitivity of the English hierarchy, but it is always necessary to remember that the Great Awakening, like Methodism, was the fruit of a continuous spiritual tradition within the Church of England. The emotional intensity of the Great Awakening did nothing to help orthodox churchmanship in general, but in particular instances it was certainly directly or indirectly responsible for the Church's gaining some of her most useful servants in the colonies.

The spiritual lethargy that characterized the materially prosperous England of the eighteenth century seriously affected the Church in America. The Bishop of London had long ago been recognized as the officer particularly responsible for the colonial Church. No clergyman could take a regular assignment in the colonies without his certificate of ordination. And without bishops on this side of the Atlantic, no American could be ordained unless he made the long and hazardous journey to England. Nor could the rite of confirmation be administered to Americans, for there were no bishops here to perform it.

In the circumstances it was remarkable that the S.P.G. was able to continue such vigorous activities in the American colonies. Talbot's lifelong request for an American episcopate was only one among innumerable other similar petitions made by individuals, groups, and voluntary conventions of the clergy during the three-quarters of a century before the War of Independence. Within the Anglican Church in America, Virginia was the only colony in which there seems to have been any considerable opposition to the idea. The Society was deeply aware of the necessity of having bishops in the New World, but the Whig politicians, conniving with the Dissenters of New England and Pennsylvania, succeeded in preventing this until after the American Revolution.

In spite of these difficulties, Anglicanism slowly spread north and south from its first establishment in the Chesapeake Bay region until, by the outbreak of the Revolution, it occupied an important place in the colonies from New Hampshire to South Carolina. Obviously the adaptation of the Establishment to the various colonies in North America varied widely with the nature and temper of the local government. In contrast to Virginia, where Anglicanism enjoyed a privileged position as the regularly established Church, the Massachusetts Bay Colony for many years was able to drive from the colony any minister who used the Prayer Book or defended Anglican principles or practice and thus did not meet strict Puritan religious standards. The varieties of modified ecclesiastical structure that fell between these two extremes in other sections of the country are described in some detail in later chapters.

Early Anglican parishes in colonial America should not be thought of as exactly duplicating conditions in the mother country. Corporate religious life was influenced not only by the absence of a resident episcopate and the scarcity of funds, but by the very nature of the frontier. The self-reliance that was a characteristic of the pioneer life and the influence of the strong dissenting groups in most colonies inevitably affected the Anglican Church, and it began early to exhibit certain particularly American characteristics. At the same time, the Church of England, transplanted to the colonies, maintained institutions and forms of worship that kept alive in many people not only a consciousness of kinship with European civilization, but a respect for authority, which they carried over from their religion into their political and social philosophy.

THE PROTESTANT EPISCOPAL CHURCH IN THE UNITED STATES

The natural identification of the Church of England with the monarchy very nearly brought it to an untimely end in America. While the real issues of the Revolution were not matters in which the Church had any direct concern, inevitably the war had a profound effect upon it. As a result of some of the influences mentioned in the preceding paragraphs, the Church had come to be identified to a considerable degree with the upper classes. Crown officials, rich merchants, and planters were among its strongest supporters. Most of the missionaries of the Society for the Propagation of the Gospel were High Churchmen and thus were associated in the popular mind with attachment to the Crown. Moreover, their missionary work had been mostly subsidized by English funds and the parishes were under the jurisdiction of the Bishop of London. None of these factors made for popular support.

Inevitably both clergy and laity took sides according to their individual convictions. It is probable that most of the ministers would have preferred to remain neutral, but this was obviously impossible. In general, it might be said that in New England most of the clergy were Loyalists while in the South the majority were Revolutionists—except in colonies where the Society for the Propagation of the Gospel still furnished missionaries. In the Middle Colonies the clergy were divided, but the larger number remained loyal to the Crown.[14] There were, of course, exceptions to the general rule in all areas. Subject to similar influences, their parishioners tended to fall into a similar pattern. In the South, a large percentage of the most influential members of the Church, the planters, favored independence. In New England and the Middle Colonies, although the richest merchants tended to have Loyalist sentiments, members of the upper class who espoused the rebellion naturally fell into positions of leadership among their less prosperous compatriots in the community. As a result, a large number of churchmen came to positions of influence even in colonies where the majority of the Church's supporters were Tories. Despite the curious contradictions of the situation, it may be said that the principal leadership of the revolutionary cause came out of the colonial Church. Indeed not only Washington, but two-thirds of the signers of the Declaration of Independence were churchmen.[15]

Nevertheless when the war was over the American Church found herself cut off from her mother Church and completely disorganized. The Society for the Propagation of the Gospel had withdrawn its funds. State support in the South was terminated. The glebes were confiscated. Many churches had been burned or pillaged, and many of the ablest clergy had fled or had been driven from the country. In short, the Church had experienced another social revolution. She was again to rise phoenix-like from the flames.

In spite of all, within seven years after the end of the war, the spirit of local initiative and responsibility that had developed within the Church of England under American frontier conditions had proved itself. American Episcopalians had brought into being a daughter Church outside the British Isles which was at the same time a free and independent Church. It was to be the first of many similar autonomous Anglican Churches in various parts of the world.

Dr. Seabury had, at the request of the clergy of Connecticut, gone to England to seek consecration. This was refused in England but given in Scotland in 1784.

The legal obstacles that had made Seabury's consecration impossible at the hands of the English archbishops clarified the need for action, and by 1787 Parliament had been persuaded to pass the necessary enabling legislation to allow American bishops to be consecrated without taking the oath of allegiance to the king. As a result the Reverend William White of Pennsylvania and the Reverend Samuel Provoost of New York were consecrated in the Chapel of Lambeth Palace 4 February 1787 by the Archbishop of Canterbury, the Archbishop of York, the Bishop of Bath and Wells, and the Bishop of Peterborough. In 1790 the Reverend James Madison was consecrated Bishop of Virginia by the English bishops.

At the General Convention of 1789 the work of reorganizing the Church within a framework of national unity was finally achieved. It was the unanimous decision of the Convention 'that the consecration of the Right Reverend Dr. Seabury to the episcopal office is valid,' and that a complete order of bishops, derived from England and Scotland, now existed in the United States.[16] The bishops became a separate house of the new ecclesiastical government and the other essential features of organization of the Protestant Episcopal Church in the United States, as it is today, were approved through adoption of a constitution and canons. In effect, the Protestant Episcopal Church in the United States, like the nation itself, had become a federal union of state units, each of which had a certain amount of individual autonomy and all of which were bound together by allegiance to a common constitution adopted by elected representatives. Under this constitution a national synod or General Convention was to meet periodically to deliberate on the general work and welfare of the Church.

After four years of work an American Book of Common Prayer was adopted by the House of Bishops and the House of Clerical and Lay Deputies for use from the first day of October 1790. It was a revision of the English Book of 1662, enriched by the Office for Holy Communion prepared by Bishop Seabury in accordance with his promises to the Non-Jurors.

With the task of organization completed, the American Church entered a period of relative inactivity for approximately two decades. It was an era characterized by the bitter partisan politics and social conflicts that mark the establishment of any new national entity. Within the Church, diocesan conventions met irregularly, and the Methodist movement finally broke off into a separate and independent denomination. It may be considered, however, as a period of consolidation in which the Church, although struggling, managed to hold its own. At the end of its first two hundred years in America the Protestant Episcopal Church was firmly established and was well on the way toward the great advances of the nineteenth century.

The buildings that follow will be the best illustration of the American Prayer Book's statement that 'This Church is far from intending to depart from the Church of England in any essential point of doctrine, discipline, or worship; or further than legal circumstances require.'

2. Seal of The Society for the Propagation of the Gospel

3. *William Laud* (1573–1644)

Archbishop of Canterbury, 1633–1644 (from a copy by Henry Stone of the original portrait by Anthony Van Dyck, Lambeth Palace).

4. *Samuel Seabury, D.D.* (1729–96)

First bishop of Connecticut and Rhode Island, 1784–96 (from an early lithograph after the portrait by Benjamin West).

5. *Willaim White, D.D.* (1748–1836)

Eighth rector of Christ Church in Philadelphia, first bishop of Pennsylvania, 1787–1836 (from a contemporary lithograph after the portrait by Thomas Sully, The College of Preachers, Washington Cathedral).

6. *Samuel Provoost, D.D.* (1742–1815)

Fifth rector of the Parish of Trinity Church in the City of New York, first bishop of New York, 1787–1815 (from a portrait by Thomas S. Duché owned by the New-York Historical Society).

II

Church Interiors and Their Ornaments

THE ARCHITECTURAL SETTING of Anglican worship in America during the colonial and early Federal periods was a direct result of the heritage of the Church and of historical developments in England. The churches pictured later in the book are as they are because events and influences in the mother country were widely and directly reflected in colonial life. In the first place, the Anglican liturgy, as set forth in canon law, required a certain uniformity of architectural treatment. Moreover, the colonist who belonged to the Church of England generally set great store on things as they were at home or at least as he remembered them to be. Thus, American church usage and architecture were likely to mirror English prototypes, although frequently with some time lag.

Early American Episcopal churches of the period from 1607 to 1807 were essentially English in feeling. At the same time, they were expressions of the culture and economy of the colonial community in which they were built. They are far simpler in architecture, furniture, and ornament than contemporary English churches, yet, on the other hand, their interiors are more elaborate than those of the meeting-houses of the Puritans or any of the Free Churches in America at that time.

In all of these churches the basic furnishings are the same as in seventeenth- or eighteenth-century English churches, although simpler in form. A wooden altar is placed within a railed chancel at the east end. Usually the Decalogue, Apostles' Creed, and Lord's Prayer are painted on tablets within the chancel. In addition to the high pulpit placed near the people, a reading desk is provided, and usually a font stands within the church building. Pews are, or were originally, of the high, square type. Beyond these basic similarities, the size of the structure, location of the pulpit, the nature and richness of its adornment all reflect the tastes, economic status, and character of the local community, as well as the materials with which its craftsmen were accustomed to work.

When the post-Reformation Church of England decided to use a liturgy in the vernacular, it was faced with a weighty practical problem. The Book of Common Prayer presupposes that the congregation will take an active part in the service, intelligently following the action of the priest at the altar. Yet this return to the corporate worship of the early Church was extremely difficult in the average medieval English parish church, which was broken up into so many individual compartments that it was difficult for the worshiper to see or hear more than a relatively small part of the splendid and mysterious rite of the Mass.[1] Characteristic of the medieval English church was a long chancel or choir designed primarily for the parochial or monastic clergy and the chantry priests, and not for singers or layman. This portion of the structure was separated from the nave, where the laity usually worshiped, by a carved rood screen and often by a wooden or plaster partition over it, painted with a representation of the Last Judgment, to form a background for the great rood or crucifix flanked by Our Lady and St. John. Moreover, much of the available space in the nave was taken up by chantry chapels with the individual altars shielded from the people by their own parclose screens. It is evident that the great unbroken vistas, commonly associated with medieval English cathedrals and parish churches, in great part are actually the products of mid-nineteenth century Victorian restoration and not of the Middle Ages.[2]

Obviously, such structures, beautiful as they may have been, were singularly unsuited to the reformed services. The only practical course of action open to the ecclesiastical authorities was to rearrange the service from a functional point of view. Hence, according to the 1549 Prayer Book, the priest was to take Matins and Evensong from the choir, but he was directed to read the lessons 'standing and turnying hym so as he maye beste be hearde of all, such as be present.' The 1552 Book extended this principle by stating that the Morning or Evening Prayer should be used in that part of the church, chapel, or chancel, where the people could best hear the minister.

The difficulty of following a celebration of the Eucharist at the high altar of a medieval church was somewhat obviated by the rubrics of the Prayer Book of 1549, which provided that the communicants should move into the chancel during the offertory to place their offerings in 'the poor mens box,' and should 'tarry still in the quire' for the rest of the service. The tearing down of the stone altars and the setting up of wooden communion tables by the Edwardian reformers in 1550 made it possible to move the table into the most convenient part of the chancel for the administering of Communion. This was considered to be in the middle of the choir or chancel or even in the nave, where the altar was often set up table-wise with its short ends east and west. The communicants still moved up to the detached table at the offertory, but they now knelt around it.[3]

When the Prayer Book was restored under Elizabeth, the division of the church into nave and chancel was maintained, but the chancel screen was retained only up to the rood loft. Above this 'partition' the loft, rood, and attendant figures were removed. The minister was to continue to read Morning and Evening Prayer from the nave, but the 'holy table' was to stand where the stone altar had stood against the east wall of the chancel. The 1559 Prayer Book ordered it to be covered with a fair linen cloth for the

Eucharist and the royal order of 1561 stipulated that between services the table should be covered with 'silk, buckram, or such like.' During the Communion, however, the altar table might be moved temporarily into the middle of the chancel, 'whereby the minister may be more conveniently heard . . . and the communicants also more conveniently and in more number communicate . . .'[4]

In spite of some concessions to conservative practice, austerity remained the rule under Elizabeth, and the only decorations allowed in churches were those afforded by the stained-glass windows, which in large part had escaped destruction, and the royal arms, the tables of the Decalogue over the altar, and other texts.[5]

The rubrics, royal orders, and royal and episcopal injunctions of Elizabeth's reign were the principal sources of the canon law of the Church of England, which influenced the furnishing of American churches up to the period of the Oxford Movement and the Gothic Revival. The churches in the colonies, however, were not faced with the same difficulties that existed in England. There was no problem of remodeling existing structures. The American churches were specifically built for worship according to the Prayer Book. Out of economic necessity they were relatively small, and as new buildings could be easily arranged so that both priest and people were intimately associated in the act of worship.

THE CHANCEL SCREEN

The authorization of the modified chancel screen under Elizabeth's royal order of 1561 resulted in the retention of the pre-Reformation screens by the majority of medieval churches in England. Where the screens had been removed or when they were needed in new buildings they continued to be installed almost up to the time of the Oxford Movement.[6] During the Laudian period, in particular, they were considered functionally important, and some notable English examples were set up. They served to shut off the chancel and afforded a separate place for the celebration of the Communion by both priest and people. In spite of their wide use in England, their employment in America appears to have been confined to Virginia. A French traveler, M. Moreau de Saint-Mery, visiting Trinity Church, Portsmouth, as late as 1793, records the existence of such a screen separating the chancel from the body of the church. It was probably paneled to pew height and above this level was made up of closely spaced, turned balusters supporting a cornice and containing an open doorway into the choir or chancel area. The three church buildings of Middlesex County, Virginia, ordered in 1710, were originally provided, according to specifications, with a 'comenable screen to divide the Church from the Chancell.' The first 'upper chapel' of Middlesex County, which had been built in 1667, had a similar screen.[7] The fact that both this building and the mother church of Christ Church Parish were built 'according to the Modall' of the first church at Middle Plantation may imply that the latter too had such a chancel screen. The first Poplar Spring Church in Gloucester County was built in 1677 with 'a Screene to be run a Crosse the Church wth ballisters' and '2 wainscote double pews one of each side of the Chancell, Joyninge to the Screene with ballisters suitable to the Screene.'[8]

The third church at Jamestown built by Lord de la Warr in 1610 had 'a Chancell in it of Cedar and a Communion Table of the Blake [black] walnut, and all the Pewes of Cedar, with fair broad windowes, to shut and open, of the same wood, a Pulpet of the same, with a Font hewen hollow, like a Canoa.' The same account goes on to say that 'his Lordship hath his seate in the Quier, in a green Velvet Chaire, with a Cloath, with a Velvet Cushion spread on a Table before him, on which he kneeleth, and on each side sat the Counsell, Captaines and Officers, each in their place.'[9] In view of the number of persons who were able to occupy the 'Quier' and the nature of the description of the church furnishings, it does not seem unreasonable to suppose that the 'Chancell' of cedar refers to the chancel screen, as a piece of church furniture, rather than to the use of a distinctive wood in the paneling or flooring of that part of the building.

Most early Virginia churches have undergone so many changes that it is impossible to say how many others contained chancel screens. But it seems not unlikely that such early rectangular structures as the Old Brick Church of Newport Parish may at one time have had chancel screens. The side doors near the chancel imply a relatively sizable area between the altar rails and the front pews that would have made an appropriate setting for such a piece of furniture popular at the time in England.* The use of the screen, like the buttressed walls, is one of the instances of the influence that Gothic methods and details continued to exercise on church building through the first quarter of the eighteenth century.†

THE FONT

The body of the church was the place for the usual Sunday services of Morning and Evening Prayer and for christenings. Canon LXXXI of 1604 stated that a font where baptism might be administered should be provided in every church or chapel and that

---

* St. John's, Leeds, Yorkshire (1634), Brougham, St. Ninian's, Westmoreland (rebuilt 1656–60), and Foremark, Derbyshire (1662), are contemporary rectangular English churches, all of which have the same side door and large chancel. All three have chancel screens.

† Notice the Gothic detail of the Old Brick Church near Smithfield, Virginia (1682), the buttresses of Old Wye, Wye Mills, Maryland (1721), and the many Virginia churches built in the form of the Latin cross. Bruton Church (1711) is a fine example.

it should 'be set up in the ancient usual places' near the door, as a reminder that baptism is the entrance to the Christian life. With occasional exceptions the canon was generally obeyed in England, but American practice seems to have been to put the font where the baptismal service could be seen most conveniently or where it might share the honor accorded the sacrament of Holy Communion.[10] As a result it was almost as frequently placed near the altar as at the west door. It seems probable that the Puritan theory of eliminating the font and of holding baptisms where the entire congregation might see them may have influenced Anglican practice in some localities. The absence of fonts in many small churches may more generally be ascribed to the limited resources of the parish.

The best American examples of the pre-nineteenth-century font may be found in the large city churches. Fine imported marble specimens exist in Gloria Dei, Philadelphia; St. Michael's, Charleston; St. John's, Portsmouth, New Hampshire; and Christ Church, Lancaster County, Virginia. Philadelphia is particularly rich in good examples of eighteenth-century wooden fonts. They are provided with carved covers and usually contain a silver bowl. Perhaps the best is that in St Peter's Church, Philadelphia, which is placed within the altar rails. The marble bowl of the font in St. Michael's, Charleston (1771), is supported by a mahogany pedestal on brass casters and the mahogany cover is suspended from the ceiling counterbalanced by a leaden dove.

In some churches special provision was made for the christening party through the allotment of a special pew for baptisms. Lower Southwark Church, Surry County, Virginia, built in 1751 and now in ruins, had the font in a slip pew next to the west door. Saint Andrew's Church, a frame building in the same county, which was built between 1747 and 1750 and has since disappeared, contained a large square pew in its northwest corner, with seats surrounding a font and lectern in the center.[11] Although Trinity Church, Newport, Rhode Island, used a silver baptismal bowl rather than a font, one of the two canopied pews under the western gallery was designated as a christening pew. St. Paul's, Wickford, Rhode Island, set aside a front pew for the same purpose.[12]

THE READING DESK AND PULPIT

The reading desk and pulpit assumed great importance in the seventeenth- and eighteenth-century parish church, not because any lack of respect for the altar was meant, but because on most Sundays the minister read the greatest part of the liturgy from that point. It has already been shown that the first post-Reformation bishops emphasized the importance of the minister's reading Morning and Evening Prayer from the nave as the most effective place from which he might be heard by the people. By the Restoration and throughout the eighteenth century, the whole Sunday morning service was taken from the reading desk and pulpit of parish churches except on communion Sundays. During this period the celebrations of the Eucharist in American churches varied from once a month to three times a year, with the majority of churches falling in the latter category. However, the Book of Common Prayer of the Church of England intended that if there were no celebration of the Communion, the morning service should include not only Morning Prayer, but the Litany and Ante-Communion, or 'Altar Prayers,' through the Prayer for the Church Militant, with the sermon following the Nicene Creed.* Although the Laudians emphasized the importance of saying the altar prayers from the chancel, their views seem to have made relatively little impact on the majority of the clergy, who read the entire service from the reading desk except on the relatively infrequent sacrament Sundays.

Obviously when the reading desk and pulpit were combined in one unit, as was usual in the colonial church, the two decker, or three decker, as it was known when a seat for the clerk was added, assumed a position of major importance. The typical two or three decker might be placed at one side of the chancel, as it was in Donation Church, Princess Anne County, Virginia, or at the crossing in cruciform churches such as Bruton or Aquia. The more usual position in the average rectangular building, where there were either no galleries or a single one in the west end of the church, was toward the middle of the nave against the north or south wall, as it is in the restored church at Wye Mills, Maryland. In Yeocomico Church, Westmoreland County, Virginia, as in a number of others, the slip pews face the pulpit on the long wall rather than the chancel end of the church.

From the time of the Restoration, it became increasingly popular to place the pulpit in the middle alley either directly in front of the door in the chancel screen, as it once was in Christ Church, Middlesex County, Virginia, or in front of the altar. The only example remaining in the United States may be seen in Trinity Church, Newport, Rhode Island. Churches that have been changed, but which were once so arranged, include Christ Church, Philadelphia; St. Paul's Chapel, New York; and Trinity Church, Brooklyn, Connecticut. Occasionally, as in St. Peter's, Philadelphia, and Pompion Hill Chapel in South Carolina, the reading desk and pulpit were placed at the end of the center alley opposite the chancel. A few colonial churches put their pulpits in the center of the east end of the church behind and above the altar, as at St. James', Goose Creek, South Carolina.

The two- or three-story pulpit was furnished with every convenience for conducting the service. The desks, making up its lower levels, had seats as well as wide shelves for

* The Prayer for the Whole State of Christ's Church is the American title for the Prayer for the Church Militant.

the necessary service books. Each desk was covered by a tasseled cushion ornamented with a valance or pulpit cloth of the same color as the altar covering. These hangings were generally red, often edged with gold fringe or gold lace, although they were occasionally purple or some other color. Candlesticks were attached to the pulpit or placed on it, and an hour glass was kept at hand to measure the length of the sermon. Many pulpits were of 'wine glass' type, a form inherited from the medieval polygonal box of stone or wood which stood against a wall or pier and was supported by ribs centering on a short column. This lofty vantage point was reached by a stairway with finely turned or carved balusters, and over it was hung a more or less elaborate canopy or 'tester'—sometimes termed a type. This might be simply a flat sounding-board as is found in the earlier examples such as the Old Brick Church of Newport Parish near Smithfield, Virginia, and Holy Trinity, Wilmington, or a heavily paneled and inlaid affair as at Trinity, Newport; St. Michael's, Charleston; and St. Paul's Chapel, New York. One rector of Trinity Church at Newport became so oppressed by the feeling of weight suspended over him that he asked that the type be removed for the period of his incumbency. The sound-board was generally surmounted by an ornamental finial. That of Pompion Hill Chapel in South Carolina is a dove poised for flight, and the type in St. Paul's Chapel, New York, is still topped by the three ostrich plumes that form the crest of the Prince of Wales. The method of supporting the pulpit upright on a single pillar was a simple one. A long post was simply sunk in the ground beneath the floor to a depth that prevented any shifting of weight above from causing it to sway.

Superb pulpit stairs may be seen at Christ Church, Boston; St. Paul's Chapel, New York; and Christ Church, Lancaster County, Virginia. The unique pulpit of St. Peter's, Philadelphia, is at gallery height and is entered by a stair within the wall. Painted pulpits —and painted church furniture of all types—appear to have been most esteemed in New England and the Middle States and to have enjoyed diminishing popularity southward. Both 'wine glass' and type were elaborately paneled, carved, and inlaid, if possible, with the ornamentation picked out in gilt. The front of the pulpit proper often displayed the letters IHS surrounded by an inlaid or carved sunburst and a similar 'glory' was a favorite device for the underside of the type.

Addleshaw and Etchells in their scholarly treatment of the setting for Anglican worship make the point that the English three-story pulpit of the post-Reformation era corresponds to the ambo which, in early Christian and Byzantine churches, was often placed on the central axis of the church in front of the gates of the iconostasis, and which was used for lessons, litanies, preaching, and certain Eucharistic prayers. Ambos placed on each side of the nave were used in Italy and Spain for the singing of the Epistle and the Gospel.[13]

THE PEWS

The third most prominent feature of the nave was the group of pews arranged around the pulpit and reading desk. They were of two types, the ordinary kind used today, which were known as 'slip pews,' and the square or box pews, which had seats on three sides and a door on the fourth. The paneled sides and backs were generally three or four feet high, and their straight precise lines contributed an element of simple dignity and solidity to the interior design of the church.

The height of the pews, which shielded those sitting within from the eyes of their neighbors, was supposed to encourage prayer and meditation. We do know with certainty that it made a real contribution to comfort during the long services by cutting down the drafts that blew through the churches in cold weather. Brass rails, hung with red or green curtains, were added to the tops of some pews to increase the protection from cold winter winds as well as to further the privacy of the occupants. An example may be seen in the restored governor's pew at Bruton Church, Williamsburg.

Of course, the pews and curtains made it impossible to see the altar, but only during the Laudian period did the congregation have any particular desire to do so except during the actual Communion. Obviously, some of those sitting in a box pew found themselves with their backs to the pulpit even though the seats were arranged so that the largest possible number could face the minister.

The pews in Pompion Hill Chapel, South Carolina, are unusual in form and placement for an American parish church. These ornamental, high-backed settles with scrolled end boards, placed along the middle alley, face each other like the stalls in a cathedral choir or college chapel.* As has been pointed out earlier, the chancel and pulpit at Pompion Hill are at opposite ends of the building. The benches at the pulpit end, painted white, were set aside for the planters. Those at the chancel end, used by the slaves, are painted light brown.

As each pew was allotted to a family who purchased or rented it, it has been said that the square pew encouraged the family and community sense of the people. Certainly every member of the parish came to feel that he had his own particular place in church. In some cases, the men sat on one side of the church and the women on the other, with the older and more distinguished persons at the front.[14] This seating plan was ordered at Williamsburg in 1716 and continued there for some years.[15] Family pews in the richer churches were often upholstered according to the holder's individual taste, and the

---

* The restored 1732 Chapel of the College of William and Mary at Williamsburg (plate 27) shows such an arrangement of the pews. In this case they are patterned after the stalls in the chapels of the Colleges at Oxford and Cambridge. The pews in Harvard's Holden Chapel in Cambridge, Massachusetts, at one time were similarly arranged.

variety of different colors brought an element of cheer into the white interiors of the buildings. Some pews were furnished with the owner's own chairs and tables. This practice may still be seen in Trinity Church, Newport.

Gallery pews of the 'slip' type were usually allotted to servants or slaves or to special groups, such as the students of William and Mary College, who were assigned a large part of the west gallery of the present Bruton Church shortly after it was completed in 1716. Occasionally the galleries might be entered by outside covered staircases. A unique feature of Donation Church, Princess Anne County, Virginia (1733), was the opening of small ventilating windows of odd shapes and sizes in the sides of the church to accommodate the 'hanging pews' or private galleries, which were built by wealthy local families at their own expense. A similar 'hanging pew' entered by a private outside stairway was put up in Bennett's Creek Church, Nansemond County, Virginia, in 1759.[16]

The hierarchic social structure of the period was demonstrated in the allotment of family pews by the vestries, which placed those families of the highest rank and greatest wealth at the front of the church or in the most advantageous position with regard to the pulpit. It was, therefore, logical that special seating arrangements should be made for the churchwardens and other dignitaries of the community. In the official churches of the colonial capitals, lavishly curtained and furnished pews were provided for the royal governors, like those seen today in Bruton Church, Williamsburg, and King's Chapel, Boston. In 1729, pews were built in St. Anne's, Annapolis, for the governor, Council, speaker, and members of the House of Delegates.[17] Trinity Church, New York, in 1737 not only provided special pews for the governor, Council, judges, and attorney general but for the wardens, 'Commanders and officers of His Majesty's Ships of Warr,' as well as for the 'Masters of vessels being strangers.'[18]

The pews were usually floored with wood and raised one step above the aisles, or alleys, which were paved in brick, tiles, slate, or stone. The three longitudinal alleys as well as the chancel of St. Paul's Chapel, New York, were paved in alternate squares of gray and white marble—a type of flooring that, at the time, was highly fashionable in the richer English churches. The aisles of many early churches bear testimony to the virtues and accomplishments of the departed in the form of inscribed flat stones covering the graves of the distinguished persons buried within the church walls. The plan of the aisles, or alleys, was dictated by the size of the church and the location of the doors. There might be one, two, or three longitudinal paved alleys. These were usually crossed by transverse paved ways at the rear of the church and at the chancel end. In addition, many churches were built with doors halfway down the nave, which were connected by a third transverse alley that formed a crossing between the pews at the middle of the church. The transept doors of cruciform churches, of course, resulted in a similar pattern of crossed alleys.

THE ORGAN AND SINGING LOFT

Organs were used in English cathedrals and abbeys throughout the Middle Ages, and the number multiplied in churches of every kind during the fourteenth and fifteenth centuries.[19] The Puritans, however, would not allow the use of the organ, and Pepys' diary records that he first heard an organ at Westminster Abbey, six months after the Restoration in 1660.[20] Yet half a century later in London it could be said that 'most Churches and Chappels are adorned with very good Organs which accompany the Singing of Psalms and play Voluntaries to the Assemblies as they go out of the Churches.'[21] The usual location of the organ in American churches was in the gallery at the west end of the church, as at St. Michael's, Charleston; Christ Church, Philadelphia; Trinity Church, Newport; and Christ Church and King's Chapel in Boston. The Bruton Church organ is over the chancel, as is that in St. Peter's, Philadelphia. All these organs have eighteenth-century wooden cases, topped with gilt crowns and miters, classic figures playing upon musical instruments, or other carved ornamentation. The setting of the organ contributed much to the beauty of the church. In 1736 the background of the organ loft in Christ Church, Boston, was painted 'bright red,' and the pipes and decorations were gilded. The king's arms were placed above the loft, which was enclosed with damask curtains.[22] A tablet on the front of the organ loft in Trinity Church, Newport, records the 1733 instrument as being 'The Gift of Dr. George Berkeley, late Lord Bishop of Cloyne.'

Of course, the eighteenth-century American parish that was able to buy an organ from England was the exception rather than the rule. The first American church organ was that which King's Chapel received as residuary legatee in 1713 by the will of William Brattle, a wealthy Boston merchant, after it had been refused by the Brattle Square Meeting House. Although no longer used, the instrument is still in St. John's Church, Portsmouth, New Hampshire.

In the average small parish, there was no choir. The congregation was led by the clerk, if there was one, who set the key on his pitch pipe. There were, however, specially trained singers in some of the urban churches, who would occupy such seats as they needed in the gallery near the organ, or in a pew at the front or side of the church. In 1739 the charity scholars of Trinity Parish, New York, became the regular choir of the parish. There are records of their singing in St. George's and St. Paul's Chapels as well as in Trinity Church before the Revolution, accompanied both by the organ and by instrumental accompanists.[23] St. Michael's, Marblehead, had a choir chant psalms in 1787. The first American surpliced choir of which there is record appears to be that of St. Michael's, Charleston. A bill, dated 1789, was presented for washing the surplices of the clergy and the children.

OTHER DECORATIONS OF THE NAVE

The other decorations of the nave had no liturgical significance, but contributed greatly to the beauty of the interior. Chief among these were royal arms, mural funeral monuments, and branches or chandeliers.

American mural monuments, although far less elaborate than their English prototypes, are frequently of fine quality with carefully incised inscriptions, carved and painted armorial bearings, and occasionally a marble bust of the deceased. Some of the best are to be seen in King's Chapel, Boston, and St. Paul's Chapel, New York. Examples of the colorful 'hatchment' or paneled achievement of arms, which used to be displayed on the house of a deceased person, remain today on the walls of only two American churches: Christ Church, Philadelphia, and St. James' Church, Goose Creek, South Carolina.

The lighting in the body of the larger city churches came from one or more large brass chandeliers. St. Michael's, Marblehead, and St. Michael's, Charleston, own superb examples. The 'branches' at Christ Church in Boston and those in Philadelphia, and at Trinity, Newport, are typical. In 1727, the ropes supporting the branches in Christ Church, Boston, were painted Prussian blue, picked out with vermilion.[24] St. Paul's Chapel in New York has a unique collection of fourteen magnificent Waterford glass chandeliers. The country churches with their widely scattered parishioners held fewer evening services and little regard was paid to lighting facilities.

The royal arms, carved in wood, modeled in plaster, or even painted on a wall or panel, were often used as a decoration of the nave, although they might be placed in the chancel or over the door of the chancel screen. Restorations have included the placing of the arms on the front of the west gallery both in the Chapel of William and Mary College, and in St. Luke's Church, Wye Mills, Maryland. At Christ Church, Boston, they once decorated the organ loft. The elaborate plaster arms over the baroque altarpiece at St. James' Church, Goose Creek, South Carolina, are the only contemporary set which survived the Revolution. Many were destroyed by the Patriots. Others were carried off by the Tories. The use of royal arms in churches was not solely an English practice. They were also used in French and Spanish churches.[25] They represented the authority of the Crown over a society which found its center in the sovereign, but of which both Church and State formed a part. Moreover, the arms of the British sovereign were not those of a purely secular person, for at his coronation he was anointed with holy oil and clad in a dalmatic, the traditional vestment of a deacon and of an Eastern Orthodox bishop.[26] Quite apart from anything else, from Constantine's time on, the king was regarded as the representative layman of his realm.

In the large city churches of true architectural distinction, great dignity is afforded by the unbroken pillars supporting the galleries, as in St. Paul's Chapel, New York, and

King's Chapel, Boston. On the other hand, in the small country parish churches of both rectangular and cruciform types, the galleries frequently add little beauty to the interior. They were often an afterthought added as an increased congregation required more seating space. The tops of the pillars supporting the galleries of Trinity Church, New York, were described in 1757 as being embellished with gilded busts of angels.[27]

Normally the plaster walls and ceiling were left unpainted, or were painted a clear white or washed with lime, although in rare cases a bright color was used. For example the walls of the Episcopal Church at East Haddam, Connecticut (now demolished), were painted a vivid blue in 1793.[28] These characteristic, sparsely ornamented, white walls, gleaming in the light from the clear glass windows, gave to American churches a certain cold brilliance quite different from the atmosphere of the medieval English parish church, but very like that of English prototypes built under the Wren influence after the Restoration. Pew sides were most often painted the same white as the walls, although in many cases the natural wood was oiled or left unfinished, or a soft color might be used. The pew sides and trim in the restored Bruton Church and in that at Wye Mills, Maryland, are painted in tones of gray and green similar to the original colors used in Trinity Church, Brooklyn, Connecticut. The earliest Gothic-type structures had windows of clear glass in small diamond-shape panes held together with leaden cames fastened in iron sash.[29] The windows of the reconstructed church at Jamestown are patterned on original fragments recovered on the site. Later, this form gave way to the oblong panes and heavy muntins of the characteristic eighteenth-century wooden window frames.

THE ALTAR AND ITS LOCATION

The principal ornament of a liturgical church is the altar from which the sacrament of the Eucharist is administered. Under Queen Elizabeth, the post-Reformation controversy over the location of 'God's Board' had been settled so that for the actual communion service the holy table might be moved out to the lower end of the chancel or to the nave, where the sacrament could be received most conveniently, although at all other times it was to stand where the stone altar had stood—normally against the east wall of the chancel. This position was reinforced by the Canons of 1604, but the traditionalism of the Laudian group in the Church of England brought the issue again into prominent focus. It continued to be a highly controversial subject throughout the seventeenth century. As a result local practice in England depended heavily on the personal inclination of the bishop in whose diocese the parish was located. There is no doubt, however, that in time the Eucharistic ecclesiology of the Laudian party was instrumental in permanently restoring the altar to its traditional place against, or close to, the east wall of most Anglican churches, where it was enclosed within rails so that it might be preserved from irreverence or profanation.[30]

By 1617 a rose marble altar had been reset at Durham Cathedral, and in 1634 one was replaced at Worcester.[31] In 1662 Bishop Hacket consecrated a stone altar at Foremark, Derbyshire, and by the eighteenth century altars of stone had again become relatively common in England. Sometimes a stone slab or mensa on a wooden frame or on wrought-iron brackets was used. In most cases, however, the tables or altars of wood that had been introduced after the Reformation were retained.* They were sometimes simple trestles but were more likely to be beautifully carved tables or consoles. Until the last war magnificent examples still existed in a number of London churches.† The simple wooden table, however, was almost universally used in America, varying in dimensions from generous size to a length of little more than three feet. The original examples in Yeocomico Church, Westmoreland County, Virginia; King's Chapel, Boston; and Trinity Church, Newport, are characteristic of colonial usage. The only early sarcophagus altar known to the author to have been erected in an Anglican church in North America is the magnificent wooden baroque altar designed for St. Paul's Chapel, New York, by the French engineer, Pierre L'Enfant, after the War of Independence.

It is unfortunate that, during the enthusiasm for medievalism in church furnishings that marked the last half of the nineteenth century, so many of these honest colonial altar tables disappeared and were replaced by neo-Gothic 'high altars' of one sort or another. Even where the rest of the fabric remains relatively unchanged, the Victorian 'restorers' have usually been able to get at and replace the altar table with a pseudo-medieval box, out of keeping with its setting but retained because of the terms of the gift.

It has been pointed out that the use of the chancel screen to separate the part of the church used for the Eucharist from that used for the regular 'choir services' of Morning and Evening Prayer continued well into the eighteenth century in some Virginia churches. Another more usual means of achieving the same end was the location of the pulpit at the end of the middle alley in front of the chancel. Contrary to popular belief, this position implied no lack of reverence for the altar. It did preserve the medieval concept of a compartmented church with the choir and chancel forming a special room in which the Eucharist was celebrated at an altar half hidden away from the nave. However, as the number of communicants who moved into the chancel at the offertory for

* Wooden altars had been in general use in England during the first centuries of the Church's life and lingered in many places until 1071 when Archbishop Lanfranc ordered that they be made of stone.

† The carved tables of St. Vedast, St. Benet, Paul's Wharf, and All Hallows, Barking, were among the best. See Royal Commission on Historical Monuments, *An Inventory of the Historical Monuments in London*, London, 1925, IV, Plate 43.

the remainder of the service was almost always likely to be smaller than the part of the congregation that went home, the average person was far less conscious of the altar than he would be in a church where it was open to the view of all.

We have seen that one means of providing an unobstructed view of the altar was to place the pulpit at the middle of the nave against one of the walls. Another method was to place the altar directly opposite the pulpit at the other end of the building. A third experiment adopted by eighteenth-century architects, both in England and the colonies, was to create one liturgical unit in which the pulpit was placed behind and above the altar in the chancel, with the reading desk at one side, all surrounded by rails. While this practice became more popular in the early nineteenth century, the best example is in St. James', Goose Creek, South Carolina, built in 1711. The typical modern custom of placing the pulpit and reading desk at each side of the choir, where they do not impede the view of the altar, may be considered a modification of this earlier Anglican movement to obtain one liturgical center at the chancel end of the church in plain sight of all the congregation.

THE SETTING OF THE ALTAR

Gradually the Anglican church accepted the Laudian reforms and by 1710 Dr. William Nicholls in a *Commentary on the Book of Common Prayer* was able to make the statement that, 'Since the Restoration . . . the dispute has very happily died; and the tables have generally been set altar-wise, and railed in, without any opposition thereto.'[32]

American altar rails were generally carried on turned wooden balusters, although St. Paul's Chapel, New York, has carved white-and-gold baroque supports. St. Michael's, Charleston, enclosed its handsome chancel within a fine wrought-iron rail, as did many of the great London churches of the period. The rails of the larger city churches in the colonies were usually carried across the chancel, providing a generous area for the clergy officiating at the altar. In the simple rectangular country parish churches where space was at a premium, the rails were often returned to the walls on each side of the holy table. While this arrangement provided reasonable kneeling room for the communicants around three sides of the altar, it also permitted use of the space on each side of the table for additional pews.

Well-furnished English chancels of the period would be paved with black or gray and white marble, as in St. Paul's Chapel, New York, but the average American chancel floor was of wood raised one step above the brick or stone of the paving. The ceiling of the chancel in St. Michael's, Charleston, was at one time painted blue with gold stars, after the English practice of providing special decoration for that part of the roof or ceiling which protected the altar.[33]

Only a few parishes could afford the luxury of specially treating the chancel floor, walls, and ceiling, but almost all attempted to decorate the east wall with some sort of special feature to enhance the importance of the altar. It might be only a large window or pair of windows, or simple paneling like that at St. Thomas' Church, Bath, North Carolina. But in important churches magnificent triple windows, treated architecturally to form the Palladian motive, were sometimes used, as in Christ Church, Philadelphia, and St. Paul's Chapel, New York. Canon LXXXII of 1604 ordered the Decalogue to be 'set upon the east end of every church and chapel where the people may best see and read the same.'[34] The most usual form of reredos was a simple center panel or panels inscribed with the Decalogue, supported by the Apostles' Creed on one side and the Lord's Prayer, or Pater Noster, on the other.

In churches where sufficient money was available, this kind of altarpiece might take on a very elaborate form, with a high frame of columns and pilasters topped by an entablature and broken pediment. The frame would be embellished with gilded cherubs' heads, a dove, or the IHS in a glory, as in King's Chapel, Boston, and St. Stephen's, South Carolina, or with the royal arms. Fine altarpieces exist in St. Paul's Chapel, New York, and St. John's Church, Portsmouth, New Hampshire. The tablets were occasionally placed on the side walls of the chancel, as in Christ Church, Philadelphia, where they could not ordinarily be read by the congregation. At St. Paul's, Eastchester, New York, the tablets are set on the south wall of the nave over the pulpit.

Probably for economic reasons, the pictorial altarpieces depicting the Last Supper, angels, or prophets, which were very popular in England, were infrequently used in American churches. However, we know that in 1727 St. Barnabas' Church, near Leeland, Maryland, installed an altarpiece by Hesselius portraying the Last Supper. It was lost early in the nineteenth century, but was rediscovered, and has been on loan to the American Swedish Museum in Philadelphia.[35] A similar painting is still to be seen over the communion table in Christ Church, Boston, although a Last Supper painted by Benjamin West for the chancel of King's Chapel in the same city was never placed there and now hangs in the west gallery of the church.

The Second Church of Petsworth, once a wealthy parish in Gloucester County, Virginia, finished in June 1723 and now destroyed, had an impressive mural painting in the chancel. Bishop Meade in 1857 quoted from the letter of a woman who had seen it in her childhood, when it was already in a ruined state. It was 'painted with the resemblance of a bright blue sky, and clouds rolling off on either hand; below this were fragments of the plaster . . . representing an immense crimson curtain drawn back. There used to be an angel just where the curtain was drawn back on one side, with a trumpet in his hand, rolling toward him were vast bodies of clouds with angels in them.'[36] A bequest for the beautification of the Lower Church of Southwark Parish, Surry County, Virginia (now in ruins), was made by Mrs. Elizabeth Stith in 1764. Her will stated: 'I would have Moses and Aaron drawn at full length holding up between them the Ten Commandments and if money enough, I would have the Lord's Prayer in a small Fraim to hang on the right hand over the great Pew and the Creed in another small Fraim to Hang on the Left Hand over the other great Pew.'[37]

In the late eighteenth century the richer American churches emulated their prototypes in Britain by installing beautifully carved chancel furniture. Particularly fine examples are still to be found in the Philadelphia churches in the form of chairs for the clergy. The chancel of St. Paul's Chapel, New York, is enriched by chairs of the period of William and Mary that were probably part of the furnishings of the first church of Trinity Parish.

THE ALTAR FURNITURE

The altar was seldom left uncovered. It was vested with a carpet or altar cloth, which normally went over all four sides, falling in folds at the corners. There was no attempt to follow a seasonal color sequence, and although English altar cloths were sometimes decorated with panes of another color, or with embroidery, colonial coverings were generally more simply ornamented velvet or damask, with an edging of the same color or gold braid or fringe. St. Anne's, Middletown, Delaware, has a remnant of a satin altar cloth from the original Appoquinimy Church, embroidered with Queen Anne's cypher. The records of contemporary churches bear out a preference for red furnishings. Petsworth Church, Gloucester County, Virginia, in 1751 authorized an agent to 'Send to England for a Pulpit and Table Cloth and Cushion . . . the Cloth to be of Crimson Velvet with a Gold Freinge and Lace, to come in a Very Strong Oak Chest for the use of the Parish.'[38] In 1774 Colonel George Washington was requested to import for Pohick Church a 'Cushion for the Pulpit and cloths for the Communion Table and Desks, of Crimson Velvet with Gold Fringe . . . and two folio Prayer Books covered with Turkey red leather, with the name of the Parish thereon in Gold Letters.'[39] These furnishings were frequently sent out by the Society for the Propagation of the Gospel. In 1726, according to the records of the Venerable Society, the Reverend Mr. Honyman of Newport reported of Christ Church, Boston, 'that the new church there is nigh finished and will be ready for the Society's present as soon as it can be sent (which present is a plain purple communion cloth, pulpit cloth, and cushion).'[40]

When there was no communion service, generally speaking, nothing but the carpet was placed on the altar in the usual parish church. In some English cathedrals and royal and collegiate chapels, however, there might be two candlesticks, an alms dish, service books, and cushions for the books embellishing the altar table, but this was not characteristic of the more austere practice that prevailed in the American colonies.*

Where the communion was to be celebrated, a fair white linen cloth was placed over the table, and the chalice, paten, flagon, and alms basin were placed on the cloth with another fair linen cloth or napkin covering the vessels. On great festivals, all of the church plate would be set on the altar, whether needed or not.[41] The early altar plate belonging to American Episcopal churches built from 1607 to 1807 collectively represents a great treasure of seventeenth- and eighteenth-century silver of both English and American workmanship. The piece of English church plate in longest use in America is the simple communion cup of 1618–19 inscribed 'Snt. Mary's Church in Smith's Hundred in Virginia,' which is now in the possession of St. John's Church, Hampton.[42] St. Mary's, Burlington, New Jersey, owns two fine early chalices brought to the church in 1708 by the great missionary and non-juring bishop, John Talbot. The earlier example, believed to be of pre-Reformation craftsmanship, is decorated with the crucifix on the base. The other, given to Talbot by Lady Catherine Bovey of Flaxley in Gloucestershire, is embellished with cherubims' heads and the instruments of the Passion—the dice, scourge and rod, ladder, hammer, and pincers. Countless churches take great pride in their silver bearing the royal arms and monogram. It is probable that Trinity Parish, New York, possesses the greatest treasure of early plate in North America given during the reigns of William and Mary, Anne, and George III.

In American parish churches, candlesticks almost never appear among the early altar plate, and the best contemporary English examples are those of such special royal benefices as the chapels of Saint James's Palace (1661) and the Royal Hospital, Chelsea (c.1685).[43] However, after the first quarter of the eighteenth century, even in England candlesticks usually seem to have been regarded simply as part of the communion plate and the practice of using lighted candles in them is believed to have become somewhat infrequent except at Evensong, when they were useful in lighting the church.[44] The custom of using two lights on the altar during the Communion appears to have begun to be revived by 1815, at least in English cathedrals and college chapels.

In accordance with the ancient English custom, specially bound copies of the Scriptures or Prayer Books were placed upright at the back of the altar. A handsome alms basin was often used in the same manner.

* William Combe's richly illustrated histories of the Universities of Oxford and Cambridge, printed in 1813 and 1815, show about half of the chapel altars with no other ornament but the cloth. The others were decorated with candlesticks, alms dishes, and service books.

W. H. Pyne's, *The History of the Royal Residences,* published in three volumes in London in 1819, contains illustrations of St. George's Chapel at Windsor Castle, and the German Chapel at St. James's Palace, which show the altars ornamented with massive candlesticks and alms basins. A red dossal with the IHS in a silver glory hangs in the chancel of the Chapel Royal at Hampton Court.

The high altar of Winchester Cathedral (see plate 9) at the end of the seventeenth century shows the full fruit of the Laudian reforms as they affected the altar. It is vested with a full carpet falling to the floor and paned with material bearing a pattern of lilies. Behind it is a low dossal of the same material beneath the Decalogue in an architectural setting. The altar is furnished with two candlesticks with tapers and with specially bound copies of the Bible and Prayer Book. Before the altar is a handsome rail with an opening the approximate length of the table. A complete set of very similar low candlesticks, a *repoussé* alms basin, flagons, chalices and patens (1661), and a silver-clasped Bible and Prayer Book (*c*.1637) is owned by Christ Church Cathedral, Oxford.[45]

The parish records of King's Chapel, Boston, in 1696 offer an interesting example of what was considered the proper furniture for a colonial church of the period. 'This year Mr. Samuel Myles, Pastor of this Church, returned from England; hee arrived July 24th and brought with him part of the Gift of Quene Mary performed by King William after her decease, viz. the Church furniture, which were A Cushion and Cloth for the Pulpit, two Cushions for the Reading Deske, a carpet for the Allter, all of Crimson Damask with silk fringe, one Large Bible, two Large Common prayer Books, twelve Lesser Common prayer Books, Linin for the Allter . . . Also two Surplises, Allter tabell, 20 ydes fine damask.' The rest of the gift apparently came the following year according to the warden's receipt: 'Boston, 1697, then received of Mr. Myles too great Silver Flagons, and one sallver and one boul and one Civer, all of Sillver, which was given to the Church by the King and Queen . . .'[46]

✳ THE ORNAMENTS OF THE MINISTERS

Finally, a brief consideration must be given to the clerical vestments worn in these early English churches in America. The Prayer Book of 1559 had made it clear that there was to be no definitive break with the past. The ornaments of the church and of the ministers were to be those in use in the second year of the reign of Edward VI.* Owing to the fact that most of the clergy were situated on the frontier, far removed from clerical authority other than the rather erratic discipline of the Commissaries General of the Bishop of London, 'it may well be imagined,' in the words of Bishop Meade, that 'liturgical services were often very imperfectly performed,' the responsive parts being frequently almost entirely confined to the clerk, who in a loud voice sang or drawled them out.[47]

* In *The Ornaments of the Ministers*, London and Oxford, 1920, Canon Dearmer states that those in use in 1549, the second year of the reign of Edward VI, were the albe, tunicle, vestment or chasuble, stole and maniple, cope, surplice, hood, the bishop's miter, rochet, and pastoral staff in addition to the outdoor costumes, or priest's black gown and bishop's chimere, worn with the square cap.

At the time of the establishment of the Church in Virginia in 1607 and through the seventeenth century, the black cassock and square cap were worn by the English clergy. To these the bishops added the white rochet and the black chimere and the lower clergy the white surplice. This clerical garb was of great distaste to the Puritans, who refused to wear any distinctive dress—and viewed it as a betrayal of the Gospel and a survival of 'popery' along with other practices and forms. The cope, or richly ornamented cape, which before the Reformation had been a processional rather than a Eucharistic vestment, under Canon XXIV of 1604 was worn during the Communion by the celebrant in some English cathedrals. The purple and silver copes made for the coronation of Charles II are still in use at Westminster Abbey.[48] At Durham and several other English cathedrals, this vestment survived the eighteenth-century slovenliness, although it had been laid aside for use in parish churches and was abandoned even in most cathedrals during that period.[49] It is relatively certain that it never made an appearance on this side of the Atlantic until the liturgical revival of the mid-nineteenth century when many of the pre-Reformation ornaments now common to Episcopal churches were returned to their traditional uses.

During the colonial period, the surplice might be provided by the Society for the Propagation of the Gospel or the parish, but the minister was expected to provide his own black gown and the white linen bands he wore at his neck. Because of the scarcity of fine cloth in the new world and the poor remuneration of the colonial clergy, gowns were fabricated on occasion out of homespun and were sometimes dyed blue or gray.[50] The surplice was worn in celebrating the Communion and in conducting baptisms and weddings, but it was customary to preach in gown and bands until after 1865, and in many country parishes the whole liturgy was performed in the black gown.

The first American bishops, who were consecrated after the Revolution, appear to have been relatively precise in following the then current vestiarian practices of the Anglican Church. They are usually portrayed in the white rochet, with a black chimere and a black tippet. We know that Bishop Claggett of Maryland, who, like Seabury of Connecticut, was a careful adherent of current English practice, wore a miter, presumably with a rochet and chimere rather than a cope.[51] His miter is still preserved in Baltimore, as is Bishop Seabury's at Trinity College, Hartford.[52] In this connection, Meade speaks of 'a singular circumstance' when Bishop Claggett consecrated St. Paul's Church, Alexandria. 'Putting on his robes and his mitre at some distance from the church, the Bishop had to go along the street to reach it . . . his voice was extraordinary for strength and ungovernableness as was his stature for size, and as he entered the door of the church . . . and the first words of the service burst forth from his lips in his most peculiar manner, a young lady turning around suddenly and seeing his huge form and uncommon appearance, was so convulsed that she was obliged to be taken out of the house.'[53]

Such were the interiors and ornaments of the early Anglican churches in America and the vestments of the clergy who ministered in them. While the buildings are of startling simplicity, compared to contemporary English churches, one must remember that they were built in a new country by men who were, in large part, occupied with the vital business of keeping alive in a semi-wilderness from which the savage and the wild beast were only slowly retreating. Under the circumstances it is surprising that they attained as much of the flavor of their English prototypes as they did.

COURTESY PARISH OF TRINITY CHURCH IN THE CITY OF NEW YORK

7. *The Speaker of the House of Commons in his Pew*

The frontispiece to T. Wilson, *The Ornaments of Churches Considered*, Oxford, 1761. This engraving illustrates the type of state pew emulated by churches in colonial capitals in the provision of special seating arrangements for officers of the government.

8. *Chalice Engraved with the Royal Arms*

Presented by King William and Queen Mary to the Parish of Trinity Church in the City of New York, it was made by Francis Garthorne of London in 1694.

9. *The High Altar of Winchester Cathedral in the Late Seventeenth Century*

An engraving in F. Lancaster's *A Geneological History of the Kings and Queens of England,* London, 1683. This is an excellent example of a well-furnished sanctuary at the end of the seventeenth century. It reflects the Laudian influence, which brought about the replacement of the altar at the east end of the chancel and the use of rails and traditional ornaments. Notice the use of the Decalogue in the reredos and the elaborate altar furniture.

10. *Typical Early Eighteenth-Century American Altar or Holy Table from Yeocomico Church, Westmoreland County, Virginia*

11. *A Detail of the Burgis View of New York City,* 1717

This contains the first view of the original Trinity Church edifice (1698–1776), the mother church of New York, and is of particular interest because it embodies a contemporary vessel of the type the missionary clergy used in their trips between England and the colonies.

12. *Two Flagons Typical of Those Presented to Colonial Churches by Queen Anne*

These vessels, made by Francis Garthorne, London, *c.*1709, are engraved with the royal arms between the letters 'A' and 'R,' which in combination made the Queen's cipher. They are part of the mag-nificent set of altar plate presented to Trinity Church, New York, by the Queen. It also includes two chalices, two patens, and an alms basin, similarly engraved.

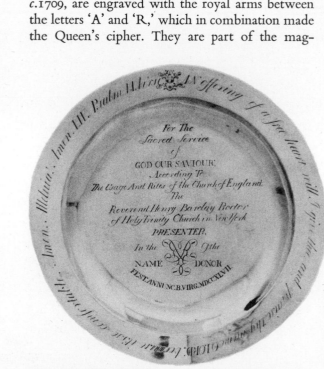

13. *Alms Basin—the 'Elliston Plate'*

Presented to Trinity Church, New York, on the Feast of the Annunciation of the Blessed Virgin, 1747, by Robert Elliston, Comptroller of the Port, 1720–55. The basin, which bears the Elliston arms, was made by George Ridout of New York, *c.* 1747.

III

Churches of the Colonial Establishment in Virginia and Maryland

THE CHURCHES that are discussed on the pages immediately following illustrate the evolution of ecclesiastical building in Virginia and Maryland during the first two centuries of the Church's existence in those states. These churches are treated at the greatest length because they form by far the largest group of buildings within the four geographic subdivisions used in this study. The colonial churches of Tidewater Virginia alone have been the subject of a scholarly and exhaustive work by George C. Mason.

The large number of Anglican churches in the two colonies resulted from several factors. Virginia was the largest, wealthiest, and most populous of the American colonies in the eighteenth century. In both Virginia and Maryland there was marked loyalty to the Crown and to the Anglican Church, along with a distaste for nonconformism. Most important, the Church was legally established in Virginia three-quarters of a century earlier than in any other colony. The Virginia ecclesiastical laws placed the vestry of the Virginia parish in the position of the English 'patron' of a living, or benefice, with the government as the general ecclesiastical authority for the colony. Actually the vestries, fearing the autonomy of a regularly ordained and inducted rector, soon began a practice that continued throughout colonial days in spite of the fact that it was contrary to English law. They allowed the parish to remain vacant technically and, instead of inducting the minister, hired him on a temporary basis from year to year.[1]

While some of the first ministers who came to the colony exhibited many of the same Puritan inclinations for which James dismissed the members of the Virginia Company, the first appearance of active dissent in the colony came in 1642, when a small group of Puritans left for Boston.[2]

On the death of Charles I, Virginia surrendered tardily, and with great reluctance, to Cromwell's Commonwealth government, yet during this period the normal religious life of the colony seems to have been little disturbed other than by a growing difficulty in procuring Episcopally ordained clergy. The Assembly, which exercised supreme governmental authority during this period, on one occasion actually offered a reward of £20 to any shipmaster who would bring a duly qualified minister to the colony, and at the time of the Restoration there were only two clergymen to supply the wants of fifty parishes.[3] When Charles II returned to the throne, the old ecclesiastical laws were revived and expanded to provide for the election of vestries that were to be self-perpetuating.

Maryland was settled in 1634 by Leonard Calvert, brother of Cecilius Calvert, second Lord Baltimore, whose father had received a patent from Charles I. Although founded primarily as a haven for Roman Catholics, it had, from its beginning, a large number of members of the Church of England among its colonists. Although it has been claimed that there were as many as twenty-two places of Anglican worship in the province by 1692, it seems reasonably certain that there were not more than three to five ministers working there at that time.[4] On the succession of William of Orange to the throne, the Maryland Protestants revolted against the proprietor, the government was vested in an Assembly and a royal governor, and in 1692 an act for the Establishment of the Church of England was passed. As finally approved by the home government, it differed somewhat from that of the neighboring colony. While the Virginia priest received a fixed stipend of 16,000 pounds of tobacco per year, plus a 'glebe' or parish farm and special fees for marriages and burials, his Maryland brother was compensated at the rate of 40 pounds of tobacco for each person in the parish and a fee of five shillings for every marriage. In Maryland, moreover, the appointment of ministers to parishes was placed entirely in the hands of the governor—an even less satisfactory arrangement than that prevailing in her sister colony.[5]

Ecclesiastical jurisdiction over the colonies by a gradual process fell under the authority of the Bishop of London, although it was transferred to Canterbury for a brief time under James II. In 1690, Bishop Compton adopted the policy of delegating that authority to 'commissaries' whose actual power over the clergy in the colony to which they were assigned was very small, and who exercised a variable authority depending much upon their personal character and circumstances. Perhaps the greatest of the commissaries were James Blair, who acted in this capacity in Virginia from 1689 to 1743, and who founded the College of William and Mary at Williamsburg, and Thomas Bray, who was appointed to the post in Maryland in 1696. Bray's great service to the Church was the formulation of the plan which resulted in the founding of the Society for the Promotion of Christian Knowledge and eventually in the establishment of the great colonial missionary body, the Society for the Propagation of the Gospel in Foreign Parts.

Although Charles II had drawn a patent in 1672 to appoint the Reverend Alexander Moray of Ware Parish as bishop of a new diocese of Virginia, it was never signed, and by the mid-eighteenth century Virginia churchmen had become uninterested in an

American episcopate—an attitude that evolved into actual opposition when the movement became strong in the Middle Colonies shortly before the Revolution. As already indicated, the result was a colonial modification of ecclesiastical customs, since services requiring the presence of a bishop, such as confirmation and the consecration of churches, could not take place. As confirmation was impossible, an increasing percentage of communicants were 'admitted to the Holy Sacrament with mean and blind knowledge, and poor notions of the divine Mysteries of the Supper of the Lord; which is an abuse of a thing so very sacred.'[6]

Communications between the colonial clergy and the Bishop of London indicate that religious conditions were relatively similar in Virginia and Maryland at the end of the first quarter of the eighteenth century. The churches were supported by tithes levied on the public. Incomes averaged in worth between £40 and £100, depending on the type and sale price of tobacco raised in the parish. In both colonies there was a shortage of church furniture, although most parishes had small libraries. Children were catechized at least once during the year, and services were read every Sunday, with celebrations of the Holy Communion usually three times a year. In Maryland, however, a few clergymen seem to have had services on Wednesdays, Fridays, and holidays, and to have held celebrations of the Eucharist as often as twelve times a year. Commissary Henderson celebrated Communion twice a month.[7]

As the end of the colonial period approached, the Church in both colonies suffered from the evils inherent in its dismal system of government by remote control. The Toleration Act of 1689 had allowed the establishment of Dissenting congregations in the colonies, which increased with the growing influx of settlers whose early religious associations had not been formed in the Church of England. They could hardly have been expected to be drawn to it by an ill-paid and poorly disciplined clergy. In Virginia the increasing number of Scotch-Irish immigrants made the Presbyterians the strongest group.[8] In Maryland there was an increasing number of Quakers, and Roman Catholicism was considerably strengthened through Irish immigration and Jesuit conversions.

In spite of the sincere and faithful ministry of the majority of the clergy in both colonies, there were enough examples of clerical gaming, drunkenness, and immorality to strengthen the distaste of many of the small farmers, artisans, and laborers. They identified ministers of the Established Church, to whose support they were contributing, with the rich planters whom they opposed politically. In Maryland, in particular, where the livings of a few parishes had increased to as much as £500 by 1775, the moral laxity of certain of the ministers was such as to cause widespread and impassioned public protest.[9] Moreover, the conversion theology, preached by the Baptists, Presbyterians, and Methodists, appealed to the starved emotions of the masses of the frontier public.

When the Revolution came, the Church found itself in the middle of the strife with something of the feeling of an innocent bystander embroiled in a street fight. It is estimated that in Virginia and Maryland, where the majority of the Revolutionary leaders were churchmen, about one-third of the clergy favored the revolt. Yet not all of the remaining two-thirds were uncompromising Loyalists. After the Declaration of Independence, a Virginia convention voted to omit the prayers for the king.[10] When the Revolution was over, the Church of England in Virginia and Maryland found herself disestablished, her clergy scattered, and the spirit of the times against conservatism, aristocracy, and indeed anything that was English. Bishop Meade says that in 1785 'only twenty-eight ministers were found laboring in the more or less desolate parishes' of Virginia in contrast to the 91 present in Virginia 10 years before.[11] The glebes were confiscated and many of the churches were deserted and fell into ruin.

With the authorization of the American Prayer Book and the foundation of an American episcopate, however, the Church began a gradual, though painful, revival. James Madison, President of the College of William and Mary, went to England for consecration and joined Seabury, White, and Provoost in consecrating Thomas John Claggett as First Bishop of Maryland in 1792. Under Bishop Claggett, the recovery of the Church in Maryland was more rapid than in Virginia, where Bishop Madison, discouraged by the unenthusiastic reception given his efforts to revive the Church, turned his attention almost entirely to his college duties. It remained for his successors, Moore and Meade, to bring about the great and lasting revival of Anglicanism in Virginia.

During the post-Revolutionary period of abandonment and destruction, which varied from several years to half a century, depending on the parish, many church buildings were left neglected and defenseless against the ravages of the elements or any passing vandal. It has been estimated that, as a result, out of 250 colonial churches believed to have been in service in 1775 (of which a great majority were of the Church of England), less than 50 remain standing today in usable condition.* Of these, only 43 were originally Anglican, so that 4 out of 5 of these early American Episcopal churches have been destroyed. Fortunately, among the remaining 20 per cent are some of the finest early structures. Though the mortality among the formerly established churches and chapels was in no way comparable in Maryland, many colonial church edifices in that state have also disappeared as a result of neglect following shifts in population and the razing of old buildings to make way for more modern structures. In view of these circumstances, it is surprising that as many colonial country churches remain.

* Mason, G. C., *Colonial Churches of Tidewater Virginia*, Richmond, 1945, pp. ix, x. Of the fifty surviving churches there mentioned, two were in ruins in 1945 and the Upper Church of Middlesex County was burned in 1948. Meade, on the other hand, mentions only 164 churches and chapels in active use at the beginning of the war.

The sites of the first churches in Tidewater Maryland and Virginia, built before the general development of roads for land travel, were chosen for accessibility by boat. The usual churchyard was an acre in size, although it might be very much larger or as small as half an acre. Some of the first churchyards were enclosed with fences of palings. Later, brick walls with round copings might be built like the present wall at Bruton Church (plate 23). The brick wall 100 feet square, 14 inches thick, and 4½ feet above ground that was built around St. Peter's, New Kent County, in 1719 had 'handsom coopin brick upon the Top and Genteely Rompt at each side of the Gates' with 'Handsome Peares for the Gates with a hollow Spire.'[12] The churchyard might be part of the glebe land or parish farm or it might be the gift of a landholder who in many cases furnished no deed until long after the church was built.

The first seventeenth-century churches were simple wooden buildings which survived relatively short spans of life. Unfortunately none is still in existence. However, an illustration in the Simancas Archives in Spain depicts the church erected in August 1607 at St. George's Fort, Maine, then in the colony of North Virginia. It would appear that this structure bore a reasonable resemblance to the early frame churches of Roanoke, Elizabeth's Island, and Jamestown. The drawing suggests half-timber construction with a filling of boards or wattles between the timbers, and a thatched roof. The church was evidently five bays in length and had a square tower at the west end, carrying a squat steeple topped by a banner and weathercock. The second bay from the tower contained a door surmounted by a triangular pediment reminiscent of that over the tower door of the Old Brick Church near Smithfield, Virginia.*

The early frame buildings were replaced in a few instances by substantial brick Gothic structures, rectangular in plan, whose foundation remains still show evidence of their buttressed walls. This was true of the fifth church built at Jamestown in 1639 and the second Bruton Parish Church (1681–3). The only original example remaining today is the Old Brick Church of Newport Parish (plate 15). The building date of this superb church was long claimed as 1632, although recent research by George C. Mason and the late Thomas T. Waterman make it almost certain that the church was actually built in 1682. These rectangular buildings bear close similarity to some of the small late-Gothic churches of Essex. The late-fifteenth-century church at Little Wigborough, for example,

---

* Forman, H. C., *Jamestown and St. Mary's*, Baltimore, 1938, pp. 14, 30. This study of the first Virginia and Maryland settlements points out that the log cabin in its well-known form was not used by the earliest colonists who employed traditional English building usages, one of which was the crotch or 'cratchet' method mentioned by Smith as used in building the first church at Jamestown. The walls and roof beams were supported by forked posts or crotches. The space between the timbering was made of rough saplings (wattles) daubed with earth reinforced by marsh grass (sedge).

approximates the 1639 Jamestown Church in plan and size. Both are buttressed and have the chancel door in the same location. The first is 17 feet 6 inches in width by 45 feet in length; the latter 22 feet by 50 feet 6 inches.

The second Bruton Church and the Newport Parish Church both measured roughly 24 by 60 feet. Although Bruton, like the Jamestown Church, had buttresses at both ends of the building, in the Newport Church the end buttresses are omitted. The church in Newport has a west tower as does the one in Jamestown, but in Newport the tower is engaged rather than built independently, as in the latter church. The only original openings existing, those of Newport Parish Church, approach a round arch. The 1702 drawing of Bruton by Francis Louis Michel, a Swiss traveler, is so crude that one cannot tell the form with certainty. The Newport windows have finely molded brick mullions and were originally filled with clear glass set in leaded diamond panes. Eaves were plain, without flair, brackets, or modillions. The roof was characteristically of relatively steep pitch, with either a stepped gable as at Newport, or a Flemish gable, resting on corbeled shoulders at the top of the wall. Michel's sketch clearly shows the second Bruton Church as having the latter type of curvilinear gable projecting above the roof of the building.[13]

The third type of seventeenth-century church is that built in the form of a cross but without buttresses—a type that appears to have been peculiar to Maryland before 1700. Trinity Church, near Cambridge (before 1690), was originally cruciform in plan, as were the first St. Anne's Church at Annapolis (1699) and the Roman Catholic Chapel at St. Mary's, which was built sometime between 1634 and 1638. The 3-foot brick walls of the latter building formed a great Latin cross 55 feet long and 57 feet in width, encompassing approximately 200 square feet more in ground area than the brick church and tower at Jamestown.[14] Under the liberal rule of Lord Baltimore it was used at one time by both Roman Catholics and Anglicans and therefore has special significance for those interested in the beginnings of the Church of England in Maryland.

All of these seventeenth-century churches were built at a time when the medieval architectural tradition was still strong even on the frontier of the new world. Moreover, the period was one of artistic as well as political confusion in England, with new buildings ranging from the fine perpendicular Gothic work of Christ Church College, Oxford (1630), to the scholarly Palladian designs of Inigo Jones.

By the beginning of the eighteenth century a colonial style, characteristic of the Chesapeake Bay region, was clearly evolving. Two extremely interesting transitional monuments of this period exist in St. Peter's Church, New Kent County, Virginia (1701; plate 20), and Yeocomico Church, Westmoreland County, Virginia (1706; plate 18). Simple rectangular brick buildings of this sort had begun to replace the heavier Gothic structures toward the end of the seventeenth century. The buttresses disappeared.

The arched windows were reduced in width and had wooden muntins.* But here and there vestiges of Gothic-style characteristics remained in such features as the gable, which originally projected above the roof at St. Peter's Church, New Kent County, and the great chancel window that once pierced the east wall.

Within two decades were built three churches that are typical of the early Georgian period in Virginia—Bruton Church (1711; plate 22), Ware Church (c.1715; plate 21), and Merchants' Hope Church (c.1715; plate 28). One is cruciform; the others are rectangular. None has Gothic wall buttresses. The windows are tall and round-arched with a flat archivolt of brick, sliding sash, and wooden muntins. The eaves are elaborated by moldings and brackets to form a classical cornice. The roof may flare or kick out at the eaves (unknown in the seventeenth century except in Dutch colonial buildings), and while it is still steeply pitched, it is without stepped or Flemish gables and corbeled shoulders.

Most of the early Georgian churches in Virginia were originally of rectangular plan, although occasionally they assumed T or L shape through the addition of wings to accommodate growing congregations.† In Maryland, on the other hand, with the exception of Middleham Chapel, Lusby (1748), which was cruciform, all of the Georgian churches were originally built as simple rectangular structures. Ware Church, Gloucester County (1715), which measures approximately 74 feet by 34 feet in the clear, is an existing example of the rectangular Virginia structure in its largest and most opulent form. This was surpassed, however, by the new church of 1768, Stratton Major Parish, which is no longer extant. It was built according to the same general plan as Ware Church, but was 6 feet longer and 16 feet wider. Its side walls were 27 feet high and 3 feet thick, and it was not only the largest but also the most costly church of its time in Virginia, having been contracted for at £1,300.[15] Hungars Church (1751) was originally 90 feet long and 40 feet wide.

The colonial churches of the Anglican Establishment in Virginia and Maryland in accordance with English ecclesiastical law were built with their long axis east and west and the chancel at the east end. The Virginia rectangular type was almost always approximately twice as long as it was wide. These buildings ranged from 40 to 90 feet in length and from 20 to 50 feet in width, with average dimensions of 50 by 28 feet. They were built in from three to eight bays with four an average arrangement.‡ The principal

* Yeocomico Church was originally rectangular, and the windows have been changed. The first sliding sash in this country were used in the Wren Building, Williamsburg, finished 1702.

† Examples are Yeocomico Church (1706) and Blandford Church (1737).

‡ These figures are compiled from the large number of measurements of Virginia churches contained in G. C. Mason, *Colonial Churches of Tidewater Virginia.*

entrance was at the west end, usually with a secondary entrance on one side at the chancel end or with secondary doors on each side at the ends of a cross aisle, which was sometimes placed midway in the nave. The relatively steep roof pitch of the Virginia churches (with the exception of a few late-eighteenth-century examples), their high walls, gable ends, and single range of tall arched windows produce a more vertical effect than that of their Maryland contemporaries. The typical Maryland church, which was almost always rectangular, was frequently hip roofed and in one instance double hipped (plates 32, 42, 49). In general these buildings were of greater width in proportion to their length, and roofs were of more shallow pitch than those in Virginia. Roofs were often splayed or 'kicked up' at the eaves, as the one for St. Barnabas', Leeland, and windows were square headed or had segmental rather than round arches. These features tended to result in a certain squat solidity in contrast to the more vertical lines that characterize the Virginia buildings.

After 1700 the cruciform church is confined almost exclusively to Virginia, where it is found in two forms. One is that of a Latin cross with a nave of greater length than the chancel and transepts. The second type is in the form of a Greek cross, in which nave, transepts, and chancel are of equal length. At least eight fine examples in the form of a Latin cross exist.* Bruton Church (1711), appropriately enough, is the largest example of the cruciform church in Virginia—its size and elaboration dictated by the requirements demanded of it as the state church of the colonial capital city (plates 22–5). Its length within the walls is 100 feet exclusive of the tower at the west end.

The cruciform church in the form of a Greek cross was less popular, and only three examples are extant. These are Christ Church, Lancaster County (1732; plate 33), Aquia Church (1757; plate 40), and St. Paul's, King George County (1766). The first of these, the most notable example of Virginia ecclesiastical architecture, was built by one of the richest men in the colonies, Robert Carter, as an estate (or community) chapel. The brickwork is among the finest in the state, and the interior with its noteworthy detail is almost untouched and in its original condition. The two axes of the cross are 68 feet from end to end, and the scale of the walls and windows is such that one does not realize its true size on first examination.

The earliest churches of this Tidewater region were, of course, of frame construction on brick underpinnings, and this material continued to be used to some extent, particu-

* Bruton Church (1711), St. John's, Hampton (1728), Vauters Church (1731), Farnham Church (1737), St. John's, King William County (1734), St. Paul's, Norfolk (1739), Abingdon Church (1754), and Mattapony Church (1755). Pungoteague Church (1738), and St. Mary's Whitechapel (1740) in their original form would have been part of the list but the transepts have been pulled down and the buildings, greatly altered, are now rectangular. St. John's, Richmond (1741), now a cruciform church, was originally rectangular and did not attain its present form until 1833.

larly for chapels of ease in sparsely inhabited areas, where cost was a primary consideration throughout the colonial period.* One of the most notable examples was the last Spring Swamp Chapel of Surry County, Virginia (c.1750), which was built in eight bays and was 69 feet by 26 feet in the clear.[16] Unfortunately wood was not a durable material for Southern church buildings, and with a few exceptions none of these frame buildings remains. Grace Church, Yorktown (1697), was built of blocks of marl, which were cut in a soft state from the York River, and which later hardened under exposure to the weather. The characteristic building material for the Virginia and Maryland churches of the Georgian period, however, was brick. Their heavy walls were laid in Flemish bond, often with dark glazed headers forming a decorative tapestry of masonry, and the architectural effect of the churches depended principally upon scale and line, superb brickwork, and the details of their fenestration.† Window jambs and arches have dressings of contrasting vermilion gauged brick, and cut stone was occasionally employed in sills, imposts, and keys. The door of the porch of Yeocomico Church (1706) has a simple plastered ornament of three small superimposed brick semicircles forming a pediment (plate 18). Simple overdoors of this sort developed later in the eighteenth century into elaborate Georgian pediments with supporting pilasters of stone or of gauged brick of selected color. The western doorway, which was the principal entrance, was treated more elaborately than those at the side of the church. Probably the finest doorways are those of Christ Church, Lancaster County, although excellent unaltered specimens are to be seen at Ware Church and at Abingdon Church (plates 21, 33, 38). In the later eighteenth-century churches of the Potomac region, cut native stone was increasingly substituted for brick trim in corner quoins, keystones over windows, and doorway ornamentation. The two most elaborate classic doorways of this later type are at Aquia Church (1757; plate 40) and at Pohick Church (1769; plate 48). The doors were of heavy, many-paneled Georgian type. Maryland churches sometimes embody covered arched porches over the doors, a feature almost never found in Virginia. St. John's, Broad Creek, and St. James', Herring Creek, are typical examples (plates 32, 42).

An elaborate modification of this treatment is found in the open loggia between the towers of St. Andrew's Church, Leonardtown. It is covered by the church gallery, which is supported on two square brick Doric piers (plate 46). In the west faces of the

* A single parish might have two or three churches, or at least the main church and several modest chapels of ease to accommodate the scattered population. Often the minister would officiate at one church in the morning and after ten or twelve miles in the saddle would preach at another building in the afternoon.

† Only four Virginia structures are laid in English bond: The Jamestown Tower (1699), St. Peter's, New Kent County (1701), Yeocomico Church (1706), and the Lower Chapel of Middlesex County (1717).

towers, further ornamentation is afforded by two elliptical niches with arched heads. The design and brickwork of this church, although extremely interesting, are examples of an inadequate attempt by rural architects and masons to handle a sophisticated design. Another feature of the Maryland rectangular church, which is not characteristic in Virginia, is the frequent provision of a chancel extension, narrower than the nave from which it extends, that results in the use of an interior arch over the chancel. This section of the building may be semicircular or have a gable end smaller but in proportion to that of the main roof. A narrower chancel extension is used in St. Andrew's, Leonardtown, Old Wye Church, and Trinity Church, Dorchester County (plate 17).

One of the most attractive features of these early structures is their windows. They are usually trimmed with special brick or stone in keeping with the doors, have heavy wood muntins, and are of sufficient size to provide an extremely light and airy interior. Only a single tier of great windows was used in the earlier churches, but in the second half of the eighteenth century the increased use of galleries began to make two tiers of smaller windows popular (plates 47–9). A pleasing effect was lent to the exteriors and interiors of many of the churches in both colonies during the first half of the eighteenth century by the wide use of oval or circular windows of varying dimensions in the gable ends. Various types are to be seen in Bruton Church, Old Wye Church, and the Chapel at William and Mary College (plates 23, 27, 29).

A tower and steeple is the exception rather than the rule among Maryland and Virginia churches. It was almost never added in Virginia until after the main fabric had been completed. This is true of the Bruton Tower and steeple, built as a separate structure in 1769 to replace an earlier one, that at St. John's, Hampton, added in 1761 and destroyed in 1861, and that of Christ Church, Alexandria, added in 1818.[17] It is also thought to be true of the Jamestown tower, which was probably added in 1699 to the fifth church of 1639. The tower of St. Peter's, New Kent County, was added some time after its construction. The first Chuckatuck Church in Nansemond County, originally in upper Norfolk County, which was built in 1642, apparently had a tower that was built as a separate structure and therefore may have been added at a later date.[18]

In Maryland, a tower belfry and spire topped by a gold ball were apparently erected as part of the first St. Anne's Church of 1699. A similar steeple was incorporated in the second church completed in 1792 and burned in 1858.[19] St. Andrew's, Leonardtown, is unique among American colonial churches in its two towers engaged at the corners of the west front. Each is surmounted by a short spire of inferior modern design, but it seems evident that the original design of this ambitious project was for relatively lofty steeples of conventional eighteenth-century type, which would have added greatly to the appearance of the church. Such steeples, like that at Bruton, were designed to hold bells, while the first story of the tower afforded space for stairs to the rear gallery as well as the protection afforded by a porch.

No consideration of these early churches and chapels can be complete without making brief reference to the glebe houses, provided by the parishes for their parsons. As might be expected, they were generally relatively simple dwellings, laid up in Flemish bond, and often of a single story with a dormered attic. The Glebe House of Abingdon Parish, Gloucester County, Virginia, is an unusually interesting example dating probably from the last quarter of the seventeenth century. It is built in T form with high chimneys of seventeenth-century type.

None of the limited number of Episcopal churches built before 1808 in what is now West Virginia is still extant. Here there was less enthusiasm for the Church of England and the churches were, of course, located in what was frontier country of the roughest sort when compared to the older Tidewater area of Virginia. As a result, the first buildings were diminutive and of primitive log construction. This was true of the first Morgan's Chapel and Hedge's Chapel in Berkeley County, both of which were built in 1740 and replaced about 1800; of Mecklenburg Chapel (1740–68) in Jefferson County; and of the three churches built during 1792–3 in Brooke County. The second buildings, which replaced the first churches in the larger settlements, were, in a few cases, built of native stone or of brick, such as the second Morgan's Chapel (c.1800) and Mt. Zion Church, which replaced old Hedge's Chapel in 1815. Trinity Church, in Berkeley County, and St. George's Chapel in Jefferson County, which were both in old Norborne Parish, were built in 1769 and were used until 1810 and 1817 respectively. The stone ruins of the former may still be seen near Charles Town.

Episcopal Churches in Virginia and Maryland which were Erected
before 1808 and are still Standing:

VIRGINIA

1682	The Old Brick Church	Newport Parish	Isle of Wight County
1697	Grace Church	Yorkhampton Parish	Yorktown
1699	Jamestown Church Tower	James City Parish	Jamestown
1701	St. Peter's Church	St. Peter's Parish	New Kent County
1706	Yeocomico Church	Cople Parish	Westmoreland County
1711	Bruton Church	Bruton Parish	Williamsburg
1714	Christ Church	Christ Church Parish	Middlesex County

c.1715	Ware Church	Ware Parish	Gloucester County
c.1715	Merchants' Hope Church	Martin's Brandon Parish	Prince George County
1717	Lower Chapel (now Methodist)	Christ Church Parish	Middlesex County
1728	St. John's Church	Elizabeth City Parish	Hampton
1728	Upper Church (now Methodist)	Stratton Major Parish	King and Queen County
1729	Slash Church (now 'Christian')	St. Paul's Parish	Hanover County
1731	Vauter's Church	St. Anne's Parish	Essex County
1731	Westover Church	Westover Parish	Charles City County
1732	Christ Church	Christ Church Parish	Lancaster County
1732	Mangohick Church (now Baptist)	St. David's Parish	King William County
1734	St. John's Church	St. John's Parish	King William County
1736	Donation Church	Lynnhaven Parish	Princess Anne County
1737	Blandford Church	Bristol Parish	Petersburg
1737	Farnham Church	North Farnham Parish	Richmond County
1737	The Glebe Church (Bennett's Creek)	Suffolk Parish	Nansemond County
1738	Pungoteague Church	St. George's Parish	Accomac County
1739	St. Paul's Church	Elizabeth River Parish	Norfolk City
1740	Fork Church	St. Martin's Parish	Hanover County
1740	St. Mary's Whitechapel Church	Christ Church Parish	Lancaster County
1741	St. John's Church	Henrico Parish	Richmond City
1742	Hungar's Church	Hungar's Parish	Northampton County
1751	Cattail Church (now Baptist)	St. David's Parish	King William County
1754	Abingdon Church	Abingdon Parish	Gloucester County
1755	Eastern Shore Chapel	East Lynnhaven Parish	Princess Anne County
1755	Mattapony Church (now Methodist)	St. Stephen's Parish	King and Queen County
1756	St. John's Church	Suffolk Parish	Nansemond County
1757	Aquia Church	Overwharton Parish	Stafford County
1762	Trinity Church	Portsmouth Parish	Portsmouth County
1766	St. Paul's Church	St. Paul's Parish	King George County

1767	St. James' Church	St. James' Parish	Mecklenberg County
1767	Christ Church	Fairfax Parish	Alexandria City
1769	Falls Church	Fairfax Parish	Fairfax County
1769	Lamb's Creek Church	Brunswick Parish	King George County
1769	Pohick Church	Truro Parish	Fairfax County
1776	Hickory Neck Church	Blisland Parish	James City County
1776	Little Fork Church	St. Mark's Parish	Culpeper County
1791	The Old Chapel	Cunningham Chapel Parish	Clarke County

MARYLAND

Prior to 1690	Trinity Church	Church Creek	Dorchester County
1713	St. Paul's Church	Fairlee	Kent County
1717	Old Wye Church (St. Luke's)	Wye Mills	Talbot County
1722	St. John's Church	Broad Creek	Prince Georges County
1729	All Hallows Church	South River	Anne Arundel County
1731	St. Luke's Church	Church Hill	Queen Anne County
1732	Old Durham Church	Ironsides	Charles County
1732	St. Thomas' Church	Croome	Prince Georges County
1733	St. Bartholomew's Church (Stepney Church)	Green Hill	Wicomico County
1733	St. Paul's Church	Baden	Prince Georges County
1736	Christ Church	Chaptico	St. Mary's County
1742	St. Mary Anne's Church	Northeast	Cecil County
1743	St. Thomas' Church	Garrison Forest	Baltimore County
1745	Christ Church	Accokeek	Prince Georges County
1748	All Hallows Church	Snow Hill	Worcester County
1748	Middleham Chapel	Lusby	Calvert County
1750	Christ Church	Wayside	Charles County
1750	St. George's Church (Poplar Hill)	Valley Lee	St. Mary's County
1755	St. James' Church	My Lady's Manor	Baltimore County
1756	St. Martin's Church	near Berlin	Worcester County

1762	St. James' Church	Herring Creek	Anne Arundel County
1765	All Faith Church	Huntersville	St. Mary's County
1766	St. Andrew's Church	Leonardtown	St. Mary's County
1767	Trinity Chapel	Oldfields	Charles County
1768	Emmanuel Church	Chestertown	Kent County
1770	St. Andrew's Church	Princess Anne	Somerset County
1771	Spring Hill Chapel (Wicomico Church)	near Hebron	Wicomico County
1772	Christ Church	Port Republic	Calvert County
1772	St. Barnabas' Church	Leeland	Prince Georges County
1775	St. Paul's Church	Rock Creek Parish	District of Columbia
1777	All Saint's Church	Sunderland	Calvert County
1791	Trinity Church	Newport	Charles County
1796	St. John's Church	Georgetown	District of Columbia
1802	Zion Church	Urbana	Frederick County
1806	Christ Church	Washington Parish	District of Columbia

14. The Old Tower (c.1699) and Memorial Church, Jamestown, Virginia

According to the most recent qualified opinion, the tower was added in 1699 to the fifth church, built in 1639. The Memorial Church was rebuilt in 1907 over the massive three-foot buttressed foundations and tiled chancel of this early building. Within the chancel is the 'Knight's Tomb' formerly inlaid with brasses which were later stolen. It is believed to be the grave of Sir George Yeardley, an early governor, who died in 1627, and is the only contemporary memorial of its kind in America. Also within the walls are fragments of the cobblestone foundations of the frame church of 1617, which was the fourth. The churchyard contains countless graves, most of which are no longer marked.

15. The Old Brick Church, Newport Parish, Isle of Wight County, Virginia, 1682

According to the county tradition, the Old Brick Church was built in 1632 and is therefore the oldest brick building of English origin extant in America. When the roof fell in June 1887, it brought with it part of the east wall and uncovered a brick bearing a date which appeared to be 1632 in verification of the tradition. However, the '3' is rubbed and vague and is more probably an '8.' Modern scholarship, weighing a great deal of evidence, indicates that it was not built until 1682 on the site of an earlier church of 1632, or at least that it was some years in building before its completion.

Whether or not the church is as old as has been claimed, it is a unique example of late-Gothic architecture in America. Its squat tower, buttressed walls, and Gothic windows are a fine translation of the village churches its builders had known in their earlier English homes. It has been compared to the church at Woodham Walter, Essex (1563–4), which has similar gables and mullioned windows.

COURTESY LIBRARY OF CONGRESS

16. Chancel and Pulpit—The Old Brick Church

The great chancel window, which is believed to have been a characteristic of the several early Gothic churches built in Virginia, was copied in the reconstruction of the church at Jamestown. The lights were originally glazed with small diamond panes of clear glass, but when the church was restored in 1891–4, stained glass was introduced into the empty window openings. The paneled pulpit with seventeenth-century detail was found in an old barn in Macclesfield, and restored to the church at the same time. It is believed to be part of the original church furniture.

17. *Trinity Church, Dorchester County, Maryland, before* 1690

On the shore of Church Creek, a placid inlet of Chesapeake Bay ten miles below Cambridge, stands venerable Trinity Church, which is believed to be the oldest church still standing in Maryland.

The T-shaped building has unfortunately suffered many alterations. Examination of the walls indicates that the original window openings were segmentally arched rather than of the present Gothic form, that the semicircular apse was formerly pierced by a window over the altar, and that another window or small door was located over the west door and may have provided an outside entrance to a small rear gallery. Although the church was cruciform at one time, the north transept was eliminated during one of the several periods of renovation which the fabric has survived. At this time the fenestration of the north wall was changed, buttresses were added, and the wall increased in thickness. The box pews, high pulpit, and sounding board have all disappeared, and the interior shows marks of neglect.

18. *Yeocomico Church, Westmoreland County, Virginia,* 1706

Yeocomico is one of the older Virginia Churches that was originally rectangular, with a porch, but became roughly cruciform by the later addition of a wing. The brick work is irregular although English bond predominates. The gable roof is steep with sharply splayed eaves and the irregular fenestration has been considerably altered. The porch entrance is capped by a quaint overdoor ornament of three superimposed semicircles filled in with white mortar. Only the altar table and font remain of its original furniture.

19. *Sun Dial,* 1717—*Yeocomico Church*

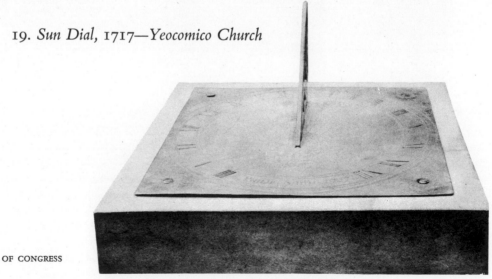

20. *St. Peter's Church, New Kent County, Virginia, 1701*

This unusual old building is a transitional type between the Gothic Old Brick Church and the later rectangular structures with tall arched windows, such as Ware Church. It was originally built as a plain rectangle and from existing indications, the gable ends are believed to have been finished with parapets. The tower was added at a later date, probably some time after the parapets had been removed and the roof extended over the gables. A door in the south wall originally opened into the chancel which was lighted by a great circular arched window, now bricked up. None of the original interior fittings remain. In an entry of 13 August 1700 in the vestry book, Will Hughes is mentioned as architect. The church is best known from the fact that its rector for forty years, the Reverend David Mossom, officiated at the marriage of George Washington and Mrs. Martha Custis.

21. *Ware Church, Gloucester County, Virginia, c.1715*

Ware Church is a superb rectangular edifice built about 1715. Its three-foot walls of Flemish bond laid with glazed headers, the fine rubbed brick trim, its length of 80 feet, and its great arched windows are all reminiscent of the nave of Bruton Church across the York River. The pair of large chancel windows shown above necessitated the use of a rather unique narrow altarpiece of unusual height. In the East end there are side doors, which open on a cross aisle in front of the chancel. A center alley has replaced the two longitudinal aisles which originally separated the wall pews from the double row running down the center of the church.

The parish, founded in 1652, gains distinction from the fact that its first minister, the Reverend Alexander Moray (or Murray) was selected and nominated by Charles II in 1672 to be the first bishop of a diocese of Virginia. Unfortunately for the development of the American Church, the charter, although prepared, was never signed.

22. *Bruton Parish Church, Williamsburg, Virginia, 1711*

This building is the most imposing early church in Virginia or Maryland. The first church of Bruton Parish had already become known as the 'Old Church' in 1674. The inscription, which may be seen today on the tomb of Sir Thomas Ludwell at the entrance of the north transept giving his birthplace 'at Bruton, in the county of Summerset, in the Kingdom of England,' suggests the source from which the parish name was derived. A second building was erected in 1683 on a site to the northwest of the present edifice. Excavations have indicated that it was of brick Gothic type similar to the Old Brick Church, Isle of Wight County. The removal of the seat of colonial government in 1699 from Jamestown to the new capital at Williamsburg gave Bruton new dignity as the court church of the colony. Although the settlements were clustered about the Tidewater, the colony, then at its largest, extended indefinitely westward toward the Pacific, and it was inevitable that even the second structure should soon be found inadequate for the crowds brought together at Williamsburg by the myriad activities of such an outpost of the Crown. In 1711, the Reverend Commissary James Blair, D.D., then rector, submitted plans to the vestry for Governor Spotswood, proposing that they build part of a

suitable church with the Government taking care of the 'remaining part—which is approved of.' By December 1715, this church was practically finished and has remained in continuous use ever since. In spite of the addition of galleries, further expansion was required in 1752 to accommodate the growing congregation, and an addition was made to the east end bringing the interior of the structure to its present length of 100 feet. The church was completed in its present form in 1769 by the building of a new steeple, which is a simplified version of that on St. Michael's Church, Charleston, South Carolina.

In 1840 the nave was partitioned to create a Sunday School room, and most of the colonial interior was lost under the heavy hand of early Victorian 'modernizers' subsidized by the proceeds of a church fair! Happily, the untiring efforts of a former rector, the late Dr. W. A. R. Goodwin, had partially restored the church to its ancient glory by 1907, the three hundredth anniversary of the successful establishment of the English Church and civilization in America. By 1939, with the renaissance at Williamsburg brought about by the Rockefeller family and the help of many other interested persons, Bruton's restoration was perfected.

COURTESY COLONIAL WILLIAMSBURG

23. *The South Transept and Door—Bruton Parish Church*

This view from Duke of Gloucester Street shows a portion of the churchyard wall completed in 1754.

Within Bruton's walls and in her churchyard are the tombs and monuments of two royal governors, a number of rectors of the parish, members of the Governor's Council, presidents of William and Mary College, and others of prominence in an earlier day. Here lie those who fought in the Continental forces and Confederate soldiers who gave their lives for 'the Lost Cause,' In the steeple hangs the 'Liberty Bell' of Virginia given to the parish by James Tarpley in 1761.

24. *The Rector's Pew and Pulpit with the South Transept Gallery—Bruton Parish Church*

Most of the rectors who have served the parish have been Masters of Arts from Oxford or Cambridge or graduates of the College of William and Mary, established by Royal Charter in 1693. One was the Reverend James Blair, Commissary of the Bishop of London for over fifty years.

RICHARD GARRISON

25. *The Chancel from the Nave—Bruton Parish Church*

The interior of Bruton Church is perhaps the most colorful and certainly one of the loveliest restored colonial church interiors, with its red hangings, gray paneling, and the black and gold accents of the reredos. It should be noticed, however, that the altar frontal and pulpit fall do not represent eighteenth-century usage.

In 1755, an organ was placed over the newly enlarged chancel. This is a relatively unusual location in early American churches. The old Jamestown font and altar plate dated 1661, which were brought to Williamsburg, are still in use. Among other parish treasures are a bronze lectern presented by President Theodore Roosevelt and a Bible given by King Edward VII. The governor's pew is at the left, suitably fitted with rails and curtains.

26. *The Wren Building, The College of William and Mary, Williamsburg, Virginia*

This U-shaped building, begun in 1695 and originally planned as a quadrangle, is described in the Reverend Hugh Jones' *Present State of Virginia,* London, 1724, as 'being first modelled by Sir Christopher Wren, adapted to the Nature of the Country by the Gentlemen there . . .' A chapel wing was added in 1732. The Wren Building has suffered from three fires (1705, 1859, 1862), but its walls are largely original and it has been carefully restored to its early eighteenth-century appearance. The college was originally chartered for 'the education of the white youth of Virginia, the training of ministers for the church and the conversion of the Indian heathen.' The contemporary sculptured figure is that of Lord de Botetourt, a popular governor of the colony and supporter of the college.

27. *Chapel—William and Mary College*

The stalls of the chapel wing of 1732 face each other in traditional choir or college chapel fashion. Lord de Botetourt, Sir John Randolph, Peyton Randolph, and John Randolph, 'the Tory,' are buried in the vaults beneath the chancel floor. The college hall occupies the opposite wing.

28. *Merchants' Hope Church, Prince George County, Virginia, c.*1715

This simple structure is located about one and a half miles inland from the James River at Jordan's Point, and takes its unusual name from the original plantation on which it was built. Its interior, which measures about 60 by 25 feet in the clear, is of the simplest sort. It was stripped of its interior trim many years ago, although the aisles are still paved with the original flagstones. The arches of both entrance doors are trimmed in rubbed brick, accented by alternate glazed headers, and the roof is flared at the eaves.

The parish owns a folio Bible of 1639 and a communion cup purchased under a legacy of 1658. The date 1657 cut in one of the heavy rafters has been considered by some as the date when the building was finished as the church of Jordan's Parish. This theory is not borne out, however, by the early Georgian details, which closely resemble those of Bruton Church and Ware Church. If the earlier date is ever confirmed, this secluded building may well become known as our oldest Protestant Church.

29. Old Wye Church (St. Luke's), Wye Mills, Maryland, 1717

Old Wye, the second church on this site, has stood beside one of the great oaks on the Queenstown-Easton Road at Wye for over two centuries. It is an excellent example of the early eighteenth-century, rectangular, brick parish church of Tidewater Maryland and Virginia. More than that, it has gained new significance since its noteworthy restoration in recent years through the generosity of Arthur Amory Houghton, Jr., of near-by Wye Plantation. It has become a unique example of what understanding restoration can do to make a little known and moribund country church a center for a rejuvenated parish life and a point of lively historic interest to the general public. This view of the west front shows the elaborate use of glazed headers in

its fine brickwork, as well as the buttressed walls and tall arched windows marking its transition from the earlier Gothic type of structure illustrated by the Old Brick Church at Smithfield, Virginia. Old Wye was a chapel of ease of St. Paul's Parish at the time of the Establishment in 1692, and continued as such until 1860 when it became a separate parish.

The present building, opened on St. Luke's Day, 1721, was begun in 1717 during the incumbency of the Reverend Christopher Wilkinson—'The length thereof being fifty foot in the Clear and in the breadth five and Twenty foot in the Clear, in heigth Sixteen foot pitch the End building at the East End Eighteen by Sixteen in the Clear of a proportionable heigth with the other building . . .'

30. *The Nave from the Chancel Steps—St. Luke's*

Extensive repairs undertaken during the 1850's despoiled the interior of St. Luke's, which has now been completely restored with paneled pews of the original dimensions and orientation. The pulpit and clerks' desks occupy their original location, on the north wall. The gallery face is accented by the royal arms (*c.*1770) in carved oak with faded paint and gilding. In the restoration, directed by William G. Perry, extensive surviving evidences of the original fabric were of great value, and fortunately a number of written records were available for guidance and corroboration.

STEPHEN P. DORSEY

31. *The Vestry House of 1763, as Reconstructed, Wye Mills*

The frame vestry house of 1763 has been reconstructed on its original foundations and is of its original size and height. The exposed face of the lower part of the chimney is typical of Maryland's Eastern Shore. The dado and fireplace end are paneled, which was not unusual even in such a small building. The present furniture and fittings, old enough to have been somewhat out of date in 1763, were given or loaned by vestry members from their own houses.

32. *St. John's Church, Broad Creek, Prince Georges County, Maryland, 1722*

This rectangular, pink brick building, the third church on the site, antedates all other Anglican churches in the upper Potomac region of Maryland. The hipped roof, single tier of tall windows, and porch are all characteristic of Maryland variations of the small rectangular brick church. The church originally had three doors; the one on the east was replaced by the bull's-eye window now over the altar. An unusual feature is the use of four bays of windows on the north side opposite only two windows and a door on the south. Unfortunately, the interior has been greatly altered and 'art glass' has been placed in the windows. The pew frequently occupied by George Washington, whose estate lay just across the Potomac, is still preserved. The rustic belfry is another later addition.

EARLY CHURCHES IN VIRGINIA AND MARYLAND · 71

33. *Christ Church, Lancaster County, Virginia, 1732*

One of the most interesting churches of its period still extant in America, Christ Church, Lancaster County, stands at the head of Carter's Creek. When the first church, built in 1670, was outgrown by its increasing congregation, Robert Carter offered to build a more suitable building at his own expense, if the old site were retained. The present, finely proportioned structure was erected under his personal supervision, and an intimate connection between it and the great Carter family was established.

As it was essentially a family church, the opulence and personal peculiarities of its builder take on special interest. At his death, Robert Carter left an estate of '300,000 acres of land, about 1,000 Negroes and £10,000' plus the unusual nickname of 'King'— earned in the colony by the splendor of his coaches, his liveried footmen, and the unparalleled richness of his apparel. He filled almost every important post in the colonial government including that of President of the Council. Three miles across the fields between the church and 'Corotoman,' his country seat, he built a straight, high, deeply ditched road bordered by two tall hedges of cedars between which his family made an almost royal progress as it drove forth on Sundays to Christ Church.

The church has walls 3 feet thick, but its massive proportions are relieved by 12-foot double doors and by 10 great windows measuring 6 by 14 feet. It forms a Greek cross with arms measuring 68 feet across. The steeply pitched roof is accented by gracefully flared eaves. In perfection of design and execution, both in total form and in detail, Christ Church is architecturally the finest church of the colonial period in Virginia.

34. *The Tomb of Robert Carter*

35. *View toward the Chancel—Christ Church, Lancaster County*

The interior of this remarkably fine example of Georgian ecclesiastical architecture is virtually as it was when it was built. Near the altar, across from the high pulpit with its gilt sunburst, is the Carter family pew, which was once shielded from the curious by damask curtains hung from brass rods like those of the governor's pew in Bruton Church. The great square pews are of pine. That of 'King' Carter held twenty persons—most of the others only twelve. The peak of the groined vault at the crossing is 33 feet above the Purbeck stone paving of the floor.

36. The Pulpit—Christ Church, Lancaster County

37. Chancel Detail and Font—Christ Church, Lancaster County

The reredos, chancel paneling, altar table, and rail, as well as the pulpit, are of polished black walnut, and the marble font, neatly carved with cherubs' heads and acanthus leaves, is of English workman- ship. The whole ensemble of vaulted white walls and rich dark paneling is an example of Georgian craftsmanship at its best and is on a par with fine English work of this period.

38. *Abingdon Church, Gloucester County, Virginia, 1754*

This superb church in the form of a Latin cross stands in a grove of great trees covering the site of the first church of the parish within the present churchyard wall. Its arms measure 80 feet by 75 feet and the walls are 27 inches thick. The brickwork in Flemish bond is of the finest quality and a distinctive feature is the use of pedimented gables. There are two windows in each side of the nave and in the east end of the apse, and one in each side of the apse and transepts. The three fine pedimented door-ways are complemented by window trim of rubbed and gauged brick. As a result of damage to the building during the Civil War, the interior has been considerably changed from its colonial appearance, though it retains much of its impressive classic beauty. The modern pulpit occupies its original location at the southeast angle of the axis. The north and south galleries were originally occupied by the Page, Burwell, Thruston, and Lewis families, who owned large plantations in the parish.

STEPHEN P. DORSEY

39. *Abingdon Glebe House*

The old Glebe House of Abingdon Parish, now privately owned, apparently dates from the last quarter of the seventeenth century, if not earlier. It is a typical example of the houses furnished the Virginia clergy by the richer parishes.

40. *Aquia Church, Stafford County, Virginia,* 1757

Aquia has been called one of the most beautiful of Virginia's churches, and, like some of them, is built in the form of a Greek cross. Unlike others, however, it has a peculiar low and primitive tower atop the west wing. It is built of pink brick laid up in Flemish bond with door trim and corner quoins of cut native stone. Placed high above the main road from Alexandria to Fredericksburg, it has stood in the path of armies during three wars—the Revolution, the War of 1812, and the Civil War. Its massive altar plate, 'The gift of the Rev. Mr. Alexander Scott, A.M., late minister of this Parish Anno 1739,' has three times been buried for safety. The high and open churchyard accented with occasional large trees is an unusually beautiful setting above the highway from Washington to Richmond.

41. *Altarpiece and Pulpit—Aquia Church*

The impressive altarpiece is similar to that at near-by Pohick Church. Beneath the communion table may be seen a marble slab, which bears an inscription, 'In memory of the Race of the House of Moncure.' The Reverend John Moncure, the first rector to serve in the present building, is buried beneath the chancel. The aisles are of stone, and a tall 'three decker' pulpit stands at the southeastern angle of the crossing. On a panel of the gallery face are the names of the first rector and vestry.

STEPHEN P. DORSEY

42. *St. James' Church, Herring Creek Hundred, Anne Arundel County, Maryland, 1762*

St. James', Herring Creek, is a fine example of the Maryland country church. Its brick porch, single tier of windows, and hipped roof with splayed eaves give it a 'family likeness' to St. John's, Broad Creek (1722), and to near-by All Hallows Church (1729). The parish was established in 1692, and its first two church buildings were of frame construction. The present brick structure laid up in all header bond was begun in 1762 and turned over to the vestry in December 1765, by the builder, John Weems. His kinsman, the Reverend Mason Locke Weems, the early biographer of Washington, was born in the parish, but the best-known clergyman whose name is associated with St. James' was the Reverend Thomas John Claggett. He served as rector from 1786 to 1792 and from this parish was called to become the first bishop of Maryland and the first bishop consecrated on American soil.

43. *Chancel Tablet—St. James'*

This crudely painted panel, carrying the Apostles' Creed, is characteristic of the tablets that were used to decorate the chancel walls of eighteenth-century country parish churches. One of the Canons of 1604 ordered that the ten commandments be displayed in the east end of every church and chapel where the people could best read them. As at Saint James', they were usually accompanied by the Apostles' Creed and the Lord's Prayer. In city churches the tablets, of course, were sometimes elaborately painted and gilded.

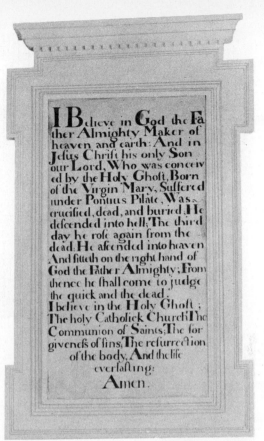

44. *The Anne Birckhead Stone*

Carrying the date 1665 directly beneath the scrolled work at the top, it is believed to be the oldest gravestone in Maryland on which the date is still discernible. Originally placed in a private burying ground at Birckhead Meadows, the stone was brought to St. James' Churchyard in 1888.

45 AND 46. *St. Andrew's Church, Leonardtown, Maryland, 1766*

This church is a delightful example of a provincial attempt at architectural sophistication. It is unique among colonial churches in possessing two western towers—which were never topped by proper spires—enclosing an open loggia covered by the gallery, which is supported on two square brick Doric piers. The corners have brick quoins which stop in primitive fashion at the cornice molding, and the west faces of the towers are accented by two elliptical niches with arched heads.

The unusual interior of this rectangular church has a semicircular vaulted nave with flat-headed side aisles supported by fluted Ionic piers. The impressive chancel arch frames a crudely painted baroque reredos of German inspiration, painted by John Freich in 1771, contained by two fluted pilasters beneath a heavy pediment. The aisles are paved with the old flagstones and the paneling of the pews is mostly original, although they have been converted to 'slips.'

47. *Christ Church, Alexandria, Virginia, 1767*

Christ Church was begun in 1767 after designs by James Wren, and the main fabric was completed in 1773 at a cost of £820. In 1785 galleries were added, and in 1810 an organ was installed. The tower and steeple were erected and the bell was hung in 1818. George Washington was one of the twelve vestrymen chosen by the parish in 1765 and was a contributor until his death. The body of the church bears a strong resemblance to near-by Pohick Church, which was built during the same years. It has the same hipped roof, double tier of windows in the nave, Palladian chancel window, and cut-stone trim from the quarries on Aquia Creek.

The interior of the church is now somewhat altered and it is doubtful that the pulpit originally occupied its present location behind and above the altar table. A silver plate marks Washington's pew, which was occupied by Prime Minister Winston Churchill and the late President Roosevelt on New Year's Day, 1942. Another small silver marker on the communion rail records the confirmation here on 17 July 1853 of Robert E. Lee. General Lee regularly attended Christ Church both as a child and during his later residence at Arlington. This handsome structure is worthy of the pride Alexandria takes in its Georgian buildings.

48. *Pohick Church, Fairfax County, Virginia, 1769*

Sharing with Christ Church, Alexandria, the honor of being most intimately associated with the religious life of George Washington, Pohick, the parish church nearest Mount Vernon, has become a national shrine. George Mason of Gunston Hall, author of the Virginia Bill of Rights, served on its vestry with Washington for many years. When the old church was found beyond repair in 1769, Washington and Mason were appointed with George William Fairfax of Belvoir as members of the building committee for the present Georgian structure. When Mason and others proposed that the old location be used, Washington was a leader of the oppo-

sition, which was successful in persuading the vestry to build on a new site accessible to more persons living in the Potomac end of Truro Parish.

Like those of Aquia Church, Pohick's brick walls are accented with finely cut, stone ornament. The door trim is among the most elaborate used in Virginia churches, which are known for their doorways. The church was abandoned for over half a century but has been gradually restored to its eighteenth-century beauty. Today, its white pancling, red hangings, and buff walls give the interior unusual brilliance. Although there are two tiers of windows, the gallery and organ are later additions.

49. *St. Barnabas' Church, Leeland, Prince Georges County, Maryland,* 1772

St. Barnabas', although of similar size and rectangular form, is distinguished from Pohick by its general severity of treatment and unusual double-hipped roof.

The original altarpiece, a Last Supper painted by Hesselius in 1721–2, is the first religious painting known to have been done to order in the English colonies. It disappeared mysteriously in 1812 and was not recovered for many years. Just before the Revolution, the rector, the Reverend Jonathan Boucher, who was then tutoring Washington's stepson, Jackie Custis, and Charles, son of Benedict Calvert, gained notoriety by his ardent Tory opinions and his brawling. Early in 1775 he left St. Barnabas' to become curate to his brother-in-law, Henry Addison, at St. John's, Broad Creek, where for six months he took the service with a brace of loaded pistols on the cushion.

The detached belfry, which may be seen beside the church, was erected in memory of Dr. John Contee Fairfax, of near-by 'Northampton,' who in 1869 succeeded to the title as eleventh Baron Fairfax of Cameron. Unfortunately the original windows have been replaced by inappropriate stained glass.

IV

Churches of the Colonial Establishment
in the Carolinas

JOHN LOCKE, the philosopher, provided the new colony of South Carolina, founded in 1670, with an elaborate system of government which stipulated religious toleration similar to that in early Maryland, while it provided for public support of the Church of England. The first Episcopal clergyman who came to Charleston in 1681 was never widely accepted, however, and the mélange of Anglicans, Huguenots, and Dissenters who first settled Ashley's colony were involved in a struggle for supremacy for some years. In the end, a group of West Indies planters, who had settled around Goose Creek, finally emerged as the victorious church party in 1796 with the Establishment Act of that year. It resulted in the division of the low country into parishes, the building of the first churches and chapels of ease, the use of the Prayer Book in all churches, the payment of clerical salaries out of the public treasury, and the election of the ministers by the freeholders of each parish. The rector at Charleston was to be given the same £150 that he was currently receiving and other ministers were to be paid £50 per annum in colonial currency.[1] Although the Church was thus 'established' as in Virginia and Maryland, the colony at first turned to the Society for the Propagation of the Gospel for its clergy. One of the first acts of the Bishop of London was to send over Gideon Johnston to be his commissary as well as the rector at Charleston.

A few years after the passage of the Establishment Act, however, the Dissenters gained control of the Assembly for a time. A number of laws were passed that weakened the position of the Established Church, and finally in 1720 the colonists revolted against the proprietary. The English government used this incident as an excuse to revoke the proprietary charter and to send out the seasoned and able colonial administrator, Francis Nicholson, to restore order and consolidate the government. The new Governor in previous tours of duty in Maryland, Virginia, New England, and New Jersey had shown himself to be one of the really great supporters and benefactors of the Church in America. The Reverend John Talbot of New Jersey once wrote of him to the S.P.G., 'all that love ye church of England are fond of Gov'r Nicholson who is a true Son or rather a Nursing Father of her in America.'[2] In any event, Nicholson lost no time in increasing the salaries of the clergy outside of Charleston to the equivalent of about £80 sterling.[3]

In their replies to the general colonial inquiry made by the Bishop of London in 1724, the eight clergymen then in South Carolina revealed ecclesiastical usages very similar to those then prevalent in Virginia and Maryland, although the Reverend Alexander Garden, who was the third and last commissary as well as rector at Charleston, read services three times weekly and celebrated Holy Communion monthly rather than the usual three or four times a year. He conducted eighteen visitations of the clergy in the colony and concluded that the Church in the Carolinas was crucified between two thieves, infidelity and enthusiasm.[4]

By 1756 the prospering colony was able to relieve the S.P.G. of the support of the Anglican ministry, and the Assembly voted the addition of £30 sterling to the salaries of clerics from whom the Society's support was withdrawn. The withdrawal of the Society from South Carolina, however, caused some deterioration among the clergy, and at the same time the vestries adopted the Virginia practice of hiring their ministers on a temporary basis and keeping them on probation for an indefinite period. The tendency of the planters to accept candidates proposed by their factors in England rather than by the Bishop of London was hardly conducive to the building up of high standards among the clergy in the colony.

Yet while the Dissenters in South Carolina were strong enough from the earliest beginnings of the colony to offer real political competition to the Established Church party, there was a gradual trend toward Episcopalianism. Although the calculations were rough and the divisions are subject to question, in 1740 Anglicans were estimated as composing 45 per cent of the population, 'Presbyterians, French and other Protestants' 42½ per cent, Baptists 10 per cent, and Quakers 2½ per cent. There were also a few Roman Catholics and Sephardic Jews.[5] The French Huguenots who came to the colony early in the eighteenth century soon conformed to the Established Church and obtained specially qualified ministers with the help of the S.P.G. The 'pasteur' of the French settlement in Orange Quarter, for example, was sent to England for Episcopal ordination, a French version of the liturgy was supplied, and the name of St. Denis, patron of France, was added to that of St. Thomas after whom the parish had been named.[6]

The French immigrants, who in spite of their political alliance with the Anglican churchmen found using the sign of the cross at baptism and kneeling at the Communion too close to the Roman practice, were succeeded by a second generation, who contributed substantially to the building of the Anglican churches and to the membership of their vestries. The convenience of the publicly supported churches and chapels of ease and the political influence of their vestries and clergy were enough to win over many new members from the growing plantation aristocracy. In Charleston, however, the variety of old congregations of various denominations remaining today seems to attest to a greater rigidity of personal conviction.

The large slave population in South Carolina presented the same challenge to every parish priest as it did in Maryland and Virginia. The South Carolina planter showed a similar reluctance to have his Negroes converted, but the work of some of the clergy in this colony seems to have been considerably more effective. Commissary Bull in 1718 reported the baptism of every Negro in his parish and the Reverend Francis Le Jau at Goose Creek was able in 1761 to report 18 Negro communicants in contrast to 17 white.[7] Bull's successor, Commissary Garden, founded a Negro school in Charleston.

Although Governor Tryon, who came to North Carolina in 1765, expressed the opinion that the supporters of the Church of England in the colony were in the majority, it is probable that, though they included most of the wealthier planters, they were always outnumbered by the Dissenters. While the Anglican churchmen, who were usually on the side of the government, succeeded in passing a Vestry Act in 1701 and periodically thereafter managed to establish the Church whenever they were able to control the legislature, the Acts were repeatedly disallowed in England for various reasons. Nevertheless the small salaries provided for the ministry in these laws seem to have been paid relatively regularly. As a result of the efforts of Governor Tryon, ten years before the Revolution a law was passed which gained approval at home, and under which the annual salaries of the clergy were increased to £133 colonial currency plus certain fees.[8] However, the right of the governor to force ministers of his choice on the vestries made the Act extremely unpopular in the colony among churchmen as well as among those of other opinions.

As in South Carolina, the founding of the Church in North Carolina can be ascribed directly to the zeal of the 'Venerable Society,' which supported two or three ministers in the colony from 1708 until the latter part of the century, when its labors finally resulted in wider public interest and an increased clergy. The great work done under the most difficult conditions by one of the Society's missionaries is revealed in the words of the Reverend Clement Hall, who came to Edenton as Rector of St. Paul's Church in 1744 or 1745. He wrote in 1752,

> *I have now thro' God's Gracious Assistance & Blessing, in about 7 or 8 years, tho' frequently Visited with sickness, been enabled to Perform (for ought I Know) as great Ministerial Duties as any Clergyman in North America; viz. To Journey about 1400 Miles; Preach about 675 Sermons, Baptize . . . in all 6195 Persons; & sometimes Admi[n]r the Holy Sacr[a] of ye [L]ds Supper to 2 or 300 Communicants in one Journey, besides Churching Women, Visiting the Sick etc.[9]*

To the south, Georgia, founded by Oglethorpe in 1732, with one-fourth of its trustees clergymen, established a church in Savannah in the year of its founding. John Wesley, founder of Methodism, served as its first rector and was followed for a brief period by George Whitefield. In 1758, six years after becoming a Royal Colony, Georgia was divided into parishes by the Assembly, which provided for each rector a regular salary, although one so small that, except in Savannah and Augusta, it had to be supplemented by the S.P.G. Sporadic efforts to bring the English Church to Florida during the twenty years that it was an English colony met with little success and ended with the colony's return to Spain in 1783. Unfortunately, no Episcopal churches built before 1807 are known to survive in the two southernmost states.

The Anglican Church in the Carolinas, as elsewhere in the South, suffered heavily as a result of the Revolution. South Carolina church buildings paid the greatest physical toll as a result of the British raid through the Southern parishes in 1779 and the two years of plundering that followed the British occupation of Charleston in 1780. Great areas of the low country were completely isolated. Not only were plantation mansions burned, but every parish church outside of Charleston with the exception of St. James', Goose Creek, where the royal arms remained in the chancel, suffered in one way or another (plate 53). Biggin and Christ Churches were burned by the invaders. In South Carolina only five of the twenty clergy were Loyalists, in contrast to North Carolina and Georgia where only two ministers were not Loyalist sympathizers.

A sizable number of Anglican Loyalists left the state at the end of the war. Disestablishment removed the official prestige of the churches, which were so ravaged or in such bad repair as to be no longer sources of public pride, and the revival of interest was not helped by the spread of deistic and agnostic thinking that came in during the period of the French Revolution. Underlying everything, as in Virginia, was the opposition of the small farmers and merchants, artisans and white servants, to the Church which they were no longer required to support and which they identified with the wealthy planters whose luxury had been supported by slave labor with which the lower elements of white society had been forced to compete in the harsh struggle for life in the colonies. When they returned to religion, it was by way of the evangelical denominations whose simplicity and emotional appeal were more congenial to their way of living.

In 1795 the Reverend Robert Smith, who had been banished for revolutionary sentiments when South Carolina was under British control, was consecrated as the sixth member of the American House of Bishops. The revival of the Church took on added vigor under the Reverend Theodore Dehon who was chosen as the second bishop in 1812, and who, on his death only five years later, left a healthy diocese to his successor. In North Carolina a convention in 1794 elected the Reverend Charles Pettigrew as bishop, but he was unable to reach the General Convention before it adjourned. The application for consecration was never renewed, and the Episcopal Church fell into a state of somnolence for almost a quarter century.

In North Carolina, as in Maryland and Virginia, a frame or log church was usually erected first. Sometimes it was superseded at a later date by a brick building, but of the five churches built before 1807 still standing, three are modest wooden buildings. The four important churches of the colony were St. Thomas', Bath; St. Paul's, Edenton; St. John's, Williamsboro; and St. Philip's, Brunswick.[10] The first three are still standing. The latter, which might be said to have been the finest structure in the colony from the point of view of its architectural detail, unfortunately is in ruins.

The oldest of the four, St. Thomas' (1734), is a simple gabled rectangular building of four bays. The only exterior ornament is a primitive elliptical brick pediment over the door. In view of the alteration in the brickwork of the gables, it seems probable that it was originally covered by a hip roof. The interior, which has been carefully restored, has a simple tray ceiling. Rough tiles pave the alleys. Construction of St. Paul's, Edenton, the second church on the site, was begun in 1736, but the building was not finished until eleven years later and the interior trim was not completed until 1774.[11] The original woodwork fell into decay and was replaced during the nineteenth century. This relatively sophisticated rectangular church of five bays has a pleasing tower and steeple, pedimented brick doorways of Mid-Georgian type, and an elliptical apsidal chancel of all header brick. This type of chancel is rare, though other examples exist at Trinity Church, Cambridge, Maryland, and, on a larger scale, at Christ Church, Boston. It has a barrel-vault ceiling and galleries on three sides. St. Philip's in Brunswick County was finished in 1765 and at one time was the court church of the colony. It was built in five bays with a hipped roof and was 77 feet long by 55 feet wide. A conjectural restoration made in 1918 by N. C. Curtis would indicate that the brickwork was laid up so that the glazed headers formed an over-all diaper pattern—a unique feature among colonial churches.[12] The east end was pierced by one unusually large and fine Palladian window, and doors marked the centers of the other three walls.

Of the other churches of the period which remain, two—Trinity, Chocowinity (1775), and St. David's, Creswell (1803)—were originally simple rectangular frame buildings, although the latter, which has been restored and enlarged at several different times, is now of cruciform type. While the typical church of the period in North Carolina might be characterized as a simple, frame, one-story rectangular building, it is also true that the locality produced several superior brick churches during the eighteenth century. Oddly enough these few brick structures in North Carolina bear a much closer resemblance to contemporary Maryland buildings than to those of either of the neighboring states of South Carolina or Virginia. Both St. Thomas' and St. Philip's were at one time strikingly similar to the low hip-roofed, southern Maryland type represented by St. James', Herring

Creek. Moreover, St. Paul's, Edenton, has a number of characteristics not unlike those of St. Andrew's, Leonardtown, Maryland, finished several decades later.

Brickwork in both colonies was usually laid in Flemish bond, the brick pattern most characteristic of eighteenth-century building practice. But in general it is perhaps less finely done than the superb Virginia work and is not marked by the rubbed and gauged brick trim of special color used so extensively further north. In South Carolina in particular there was greater use of both stucco work and wooden exterior ornamentation, particularly in cornices and window frames, than there was in Virginia. Obviously masonry that was to be covered with stucco did not require such careful finish. Brick churchyard walls were customary in both colonies when the parish could afford them.

The pre-Revolutionary churches of South Carolina have distinctive characteristics of their own which grew out of the great plantation society that produced them. In some rural parishes they are the first and only church edifices built on the site. The decoration of the interiors of the small parish churches and chapels of ease in South Carolina on the whole is richer than is usually found elsewhere in contemporary colonial country churches. Stucco work was widely used both to enrich the interiors and as exterior accents to door and window openings as well as to cover brick pillars or walls.

With the exception of the Charleston churches, these buildings were originally of single-story rectangular form with a single tier of high arched windows, no tower or steeple, and often a jerkin-head roof. Prince George, Winyah, built its tower in 1820, however, while St. Andrew's Church, which is the oldest building of the colonial Episcopal establishment in the state, had added the apse and transepts of its present cruciform structure to the rectangular nave in 1723 (plate 50). The gable ends are finished in simple parapets. The plain exterior walls of St. Andrew's are stuccoed, as are those of St. James', Goose Creek, which is preserved much as it was at the time of its building in 1711. Its rectangular mass, elaborate stucco ornament, yellow walls, and jerkin-head roof bear an unmistakable relationship to the West Indian architecture with which the planters of Goose Creek, who built it, were familiar in their native Barbados. The same affinity to the West Indies may be found in a number of simple old tile-roofed houses in Charleston. Christ Church (1724) and Strawberry Chapel (1725) are also rectangular, stuccoed brick buildings but have little exterior ornamentation. The latter has a jerkin-head roof similar to those at Goose Creek, and at the ruined White Church, St. Helena Island (c.1725), which was built of tabby or marl.

By the third quarter of the eighteenth century, the simpler, earlier type building was made more elaborate in some instances by the addition of columned porticoes. Prince William's Church, Sheldon (1753), and St. James', Santee (1768), are examples. The ruins of the former church, burned by Sherman's 15th Corps in 1865, still retain unique elegance from the half-round pilasters of molded brick which surround three sides of the building. It was the most elaborate church built in the Carolinas outside of Charleston. Biggin Church (1755), which is also in ruins, Pompion Hill Chapel, built in 1763, and St. Stephen's Church (1767) are structures of the simpler type (plates 60–64). All are of massive brickwork—in these cases without a pargeting of stucco. Pompion Hill Chapel has the local jerkin-head roof, while that of St. Stephen's is of a gambrel form terminating in scrolled baroque parapets at the ends similar to those at the Church of Prince George, Winyah, and at Middleton Place and North Chachan Plantations.

The great charm of the minor South Carolina churches lies as much in the variety of their interior treatment as in the distinct regional feeling that typifies their exterior appearance. The magnificence of the provincial baroque ornamentation in colored high relief that marks the reredos of St. James', Goose Creek, which is in perfect complement to the exterior ornamentation of the pediment over the door and the keystones of the window arches, is in marked contrast to the chaste classicism of the chancel treatment at Pompion Hill or St. James', Santee. One finds a compromise in the Mid-Georgian reredos of St. Stephen's with its gilded sunburst and elaborately paneled Palladian window. Yet the ornamented tray ceiling of St. Stephen's, the chancel of Pompion Hill, and the ornamented cedar pulpits in both churches are all obvious borrowings from St. Michael's Church in Charleston. Here is an architectural sophistication that is seldom found in rural parish churches farther north.

Pulpits and their testers are made of carved and inlaid local red cedar, which was a favorite material for cabinetwork of all sorts—and particularly for coffins—from the earliest days of the colony. Cedar was also favored for pews, and those used by the slaves were sometimes designated by being painted a different color from those set aside for the white congregation. The outer doors of these buildings are almost always of double form and are paneled like the heavy window shutters.

The later small country churches in South Carolina were greatly influenced architecturally by the building of the new St. Michael's in Charleston during the 1750's (plates 61–3). It is not unlikely that the imposing new church derived some characteristics from St. Philip's, Charleston, which had been built of brick in 1727 'with a cupola of fifty feet; with two bells, and a clock and bell' and which had 'three porticoes before the west, south and north doors.'[13] This church, 100 feet long by 60 feet wide, burned in 1835 and was succeeded by the present St. Philip's, which has similar porticoes, although a tall steeple replaces the original cupola. In any event, the earlier St. Philip's Church was overshadowed by St. Michael's, with its steeple 186 feet in height and its greater length of 130 feet.

St. Michael's may be considered a triumph of South Carolina colonial craftsmanship. It is built of stuccoed brick with seven bays of arched windows in two tiers separated by pilasters with capitals of the Tuscan order, a classic portico over an impressive entrance, and a superb tower housing a peal of eight bells and culminating in a lofty spire. Its interior trim is of beautifully paneled and carved red cedar and cypress, and many of its furnishings were imported from London during the eighteenth century (plates 57–9). The walled churchyard is entered through fine gates of characteristic Charleston wrought-iron work. Both architecturally and historically St. Michael's should stand near the top of any list of eighteenth-century churches built in America.

Episcopal Churches in the Carolinas which were Erected
before 1808 and are still Standing:

NORTH CAROLINA

1734	St. Thomas' Church	Bath	Beaufort County
1736	St. Paul's Church	Edenton	Chowan County
1757	St. John's Church	Williamsboro	Granville County
1775	Trinity Church	Chocowinity	Beaufort County
1803	St. David's Church (Pettigrew's Chapel)	Creswell	Washington County

SOUTH CAROLINA

1706	St. Andrew's Church	St. Andrew's Parish, near Charleston	Charleston County
1707	St. Thomas' and St. Denis' Church	near Cain Hoy	Charleston County
1711	St. James' Church	Goose Creek	Berkeley County
1724	Christ Church	near Mount Pleasant	Charleston County
1724	St. Helena's Church	Beaufort	Beaufort County
1725	Strawberry Chapel	St. John's Parish, near Cordesville	Berkeley County
1742	Church of Prince George, Winyah	Georgetown	Georgetown County
1752	St. Michael's Church	Charleston	Charleston County
1763	Pompion Hill Chapel	St. Thomas' Parish, near Huger	Berkeley County
1767	St. Stephen's Church	St. Stephens	Berkeley County
1768	St. James' Church	Santee	Charleston County
1770	St. David's Church	Cheraw	Chesterfield County

50. *St. Andrew's Church, near Charleston, South Carolina, 1706*

If one drives north from Charleston to see Magnolia Gardens and Middleton Place, he will pass St. Andrew's. This oldest architectural relic of the Church of England in South Carolina has a quaint severity combined with great charm. Its stucco walls, blue-green doors, and shutters gleam amid towering oaks dripping with Spanish moss. In the churchyard are a number of elaborate old tombs. This parish, embracing the lower Ashley River area, with its fine early plantations, was at one time one of the richest and most important in the Carolinas. A tile set in the end of one of the transepts records the building supervisors J. F. (Jonathan Fitch) and T. R. (Thomas Rose) and the date 1706.

51. *Interior—St. Andrew's, near Charleston*

The towering reredos of dark wood accented in gilt and carrying the Creed, Lord's Prayer, and Ten Commandments has great dignity. Now of cruciform plan, the original rectangular building was enlarged in 1723 by the addition of a chancel and transepts to the nave. At that time the tile carrying the date the parish was established was apparently removed from the chancel and placed in its present position. The building was gutted by fire in 1764 and rebuilt in its present form on the old walls.

52. St. James' Church, Goose Creek, South Carolina, 1711

Off the beaten track of the average traveler stands Goose Creek Church, one of the best preserved and most interesting early churches in the United States. With its walls of yellow stucco, it might be set down in Antigua or Barbados and seem thoroughly at home. St. James' was the place of worship of the first Anglican congregation outside of Charleston—the planters from Barbados, who were instrumental in the introduction of the Established Church into the province. The origin of its builders is apparent in the similarity of the building—with its jerkinhead roof, stucco ornamentation, and color—to contemporary West Indian structures.

Fortunately, during the Revolution, St. James', where the royal arms remained as part of the reredos, was spared the destruction or indignity visited by British troops on almost every other parish church in the plantation area. It was equally fortunate in 1865 when Sherman's troops crossed the Carolina low count

53. *The Chancel—Goose Creek*

A High-Church note is set by the cherubim over the windows, the overdoor with its flaming hearts and 'Pelican in her Piety vulning her breast' (symbol of maternal sacrifice and device of the Society for the Propagation of the Gospel), as well as by the fine baroque reredos of plaster within the church. In the reredos pilasters in the composite order support a curved and broken pediment framing the royal arms which are modeled in the round in full color.

The wooden altar is set below and beneath the pulpit and, with the reading desk, forms a single liturgical center. Cherubim supporting the Bible form the keystone of the arched chancel window. There are some heraldic mural memorials to former parishioners and on the gallery at the rear of the church hangs one of the last hatchments known to exist in the United States, that of Ralph Izard, member of a family of planters distinguished for public service.

54. *St. Thomas' Church, Bath, North Carolina, 1734*

St. Thomas' is the oldest church in North Carolina. The only exterior ornament of this simple building is the primitive brick pediment over the door. The church is built in the form of a simple rectangle of four bays, 51 feet long by 31 feet wide, and, from the different types of brickwork in the gables, was probably covered by a hipped roof at one time. The walls are two feet thick. The bell, which is housed separately, was cast in England in 1732 and recast in New York in 1872.

55. Interior—St. Thomas'

The interior, which has been restored, is floored with the original eight-inch-square tiles. The chancel is raised two steps above the body of the church. According to local tradition the church's silver candelabra were the gift of King George II. Appropriately the altar table, paneled reredos, pulpit, and slip pews are all of the plainest sort. The ceiling is of the primitive tray type.

56. *St. Paul's Church, Edenton, North Carolina, 1736*

In the spring few churches have a setting of greater peace and beauty than St. Paul's, whose green churchyard is dotted with pink and white dogwood trees. Here are the graves of five royal governors of the colony.

St. Paul's was organized in 1701 and is the oldest corporation of continuous life in North Carolina. The second and present church, built by voluntary subscription, was begun in 1736, but the work on it was so intermittent that it was not completed and services were not held in the building until 1760. Though the main construction remains unchanged, the interior has been restored following a recent fire. Colonel Edward Mosely appears to have been the principal benefactor of the earlier church for which he purchased a library of seventy-four volumes in London in 1720. The silver chalice and paten given by Mosely in 1726 are still in use.

57. St. Michael's Church, Charleston, South Carolina, 1752

The great steeple of St. Michael's dominates the Charleston skyline with an air of strength and tremendous solidity. Although the building has been attributed to James Gibbs and lately to Peter Harrison, no mention of the architect is made in the church manuscripts. Combined with the low bulk of the main structure, St. Michael's steeple attains a powerful beauty that places the whole edifice among the foremost examples of Georgian architecture in America. The cornerstone of the church, the second on this site, was laid by the governor of the colony on 17 February 1752, but it was not opened for divine service until 1 February 1761. Its stuccoed and painted brick, dazzling white in the brilliant semi-tropical sun, is only slightly softened by the green foliage of the churchyard.

The church's scrolled iron gates are among the best in Charleston, a city famed for its ornamental ironwork. The fabric is divided by pilasters into seven bays with two tiers of arched windows. The great central doorway is protected by a pedimented portico supported by four massive Tuscan columns. The building is 130 feet long and 60 feet wide and its steeple is 186 feet high. The eight bells, which were brought from England in 1764, were taken back there during the British occupation of Charleston at the time of the Revolution. They were then purchased by a London merchant, a member of Parliament, and were shipped back and rehung. Later two became cracked and were sent again to England for recasting. In June 1862, the bells were sent to Columbia for safety. They were burned in the great fire there but in 1866 were sent to England and again recast. Thus, several have crossed the Atlantic seven times. Ornamenting the white walls of the impressive interior are mural monuments to the memory of those who lie beneath the church. Among these are General Charles Cotesworth Pinckney and two early bishops of the diocese, Theodore Dehon and Nathaniel Bowen.

F. S. LINCOLN

58. Chancel—St. Michael's, Charleston

The Palladian window over the altar was bricked up in 1788 as a fire protection measure but was reopened when the chancel was repaired in 1865, after being wrecked by a shell from the Federal batteries. The stained glass, of course, dates from the 1890's.

The heads of the tablets have since been altered and a number of other changes have been made in the colorful decoration of the chancel. Its entire background was originally cobalt blue, with a gilded sun in a glory and stars and clouds in the half dome. The frames of the tablets were gilded, the lettering was gold on blue, and the mahogany chairs ordered for the chancel in 1815 were upholstered in red velour. The original chancel rail of wood was replaced by the present gilded wrought-iron rail purchased in England in 1772. Characteristic of the best contemporary English ironwork, its design is nevertheless sufficiently restrained and simple to have been readily copied and adapted to other uses by local smiths for many years.

RONALD ALLEN REILLY

59. Nave—St. Michael's, Charleston

The richly carved pulpit occupies its original location at the southern corner of the red and blue tiled middle alley, although the original clerk's pew and reading desk were replaced by the present desk in 1893. The great 42-light chandelier was imported from England in 1803. The organ retains the case and some of the pipes of the Snetzler organ imported in 1768. In 1772 'Crimson Indian Damask curtains for the Organ Gallery, to run upon Brass Rods . . . [with] double Gilt Pine Apple Tops at each end' were ordered. The gallery is believed to have been occupied by the first surpliced boy choir in the United States, mentioned in the records of the vestry as early as 1794. The decorative work of the fine tray ceiling is of the same carved cypress and cedar as the rest of the church furnishings.

60. *Pompion Hill Chapel, St. Thomas' and St. Denis' Parish, South Carolina,* 1763

Between 1680 and 1700 on the bluffs above the eastern branch of the Cooper River, a Huguenot community of small plantations was established. For the benefit of this area a wooden chapel of ease of St. Thomas and St. Denis Parish was built in 1703 at Pompion Hill, but by 1763 it was in such a state of dilapidation that the congregation arranged for the erection of the present building at a cost of £570. Of this, £200 was furnished by the province, the balance being raised by private subscriptions.

It is probable that the design, as well as the building of this pleasing little church, may be ascribed to Zachariah Villepontoux, a vestryman of Saint James', Goose Creek, whose name is also connected with St. Michael's, Charleston. Villepontoux made the brick for Saint Michael's at his 'Parnassus Plantation' on Back River. Here his initials appear on both sides of both north and south doors. William Axson, who probably did much of the brickwork, put his name with various Masonic emblems on one wall, as he did at Saint Stephen's in the neighboring parish.

61. *The Chancel—Pompion Hill Chapel*

63. *Pulpit Detail—Pompion Hill Chapel*

The design of both pulpit and chancel were obviously borrowed from St. Michael's in Charleston, which had just been completed. As is true of much of the woodwork in the latter church, the pulpit here is of native red cedar, beautifully carved and inlaid. The front panel carries a sunburst bearing the sacred monogram IHS. Similar decoration appears on the underside of the sounding board which is topped with a dove. Arched windows complement the vaulted ceiling which springs from a well-molded cornice. Both the trim and furnishings are fine examples of local craftsmanship.

62. *Pulpit and Desk—Pompion Hill Chapel*

Gabriel Manigault, the great Charleston merchant and planter, in addition to his subscription of £50, gave £10 for the red tiles that still form the alleys crossing the pavement of brick laid in herringbone pattern. The high-backed benches face each other along the middle alley leading from the altar to the pulpit, which are at opposite ends of the church. The settees at the chancel end are light brown and were used by the slaves. Those near the pulpit are painted white and were for the use of the planters.

64. *St. Stephen's Church, St. Stephens, South Carolina, 1767*

St. Stephen's Church, which replaced a decayed earlier wooden chapel, is distinguished by its baroque, curvilinear, parapeted gables, and gambrel roof. It is built on the usual plan of South Carolina rectangular country parish churches with the chancel at the east end and a cross aisle midway in the body of the church. In this case, however, the five bays of arched openings are separated by brick pilasters supporting a wide, wooden cornice.

St. Stephen's Parish was created in 1754 out of the upper part of the Parish of St. James', Santee, which had been known as French Santee and which was then a prosperous indigo region. A. Howard and Francis Villepontoux, nephew of Zachariah who worked at Pompion Hill, were supervisors of construction and architects, according to tradition. In order to incorporate a tray ceiling like that at Saint Michael's, Charleston, an uncommonly heavy roof was used and the window over the altar is too small. In spite of these defects of design and an unusual arrangement of pews, the church is pleasing as a whole.

The reredos is unusually impressive. On either side of the small Palladian window, framed by fluted pilasters carrying a broken pediment, are taller dog-eared frames for the tablets of the Law, between fluted pilasters supporting entablatures from which springs a higher denticulated pediment surmounting the whole window treatment. The space between the top of the window and the point of the pediment is ornamented by a gilded glory surrounding the letters IHS.

V

Early Episcopal Churches of the Middle States

THE STATES OF NEW YORK, New Jersey, Pennsylvania, and Delaware are treated as a group, not only because they were the 'Middle Colonies' of the original 13 in a geographical sense, but because here was a mingling of the political, social, and architectural characteristics of the groups of colonies to the north and to the south. In New York, for example, where the Church of England was partially established as in the South, and where there were more slaves than in any of the other colonies north of the tobacco belt, there remain many small white wooden churches reminiscent of those in New England. Moreover, here, as in near-by Connecticut, High Churchmanship prevailed, and the principal opposition came from 'Independents' and Presbyterians. In Pennsylvania and Delaware, on the other hand, where the Church of England, as in New England, enjoyed no special privileges, the country churches bore a stronger resemblance to those of the Southern colonies, as did the type of churchmanship, although the principal antagonists of Anglicanism were Quakers and Presbyterians.

With the bloodless conquest of the Dutch colony of New Amsterdam by the English in 1664, Anglican services were first held in the chapel at the fort, and the governor and garrison continued to be served by military chaplains or visiting clergymen until 1697, sharing the Dutch church on amicable terms that were in decided contrast to the arrangement instituted by the first royal governor at Boston. On 6 May 1697, however, a charter granted by William III was signed by Governor Fletcher, bringing into legal existence 'the Parish of Trinity Church within Our said City of New-York.'[1]

The Right Reverend Dr. Henry Compton, Lord Bishop of London, was appointed titular rector until a suitable resident minister could be secured. Later in the year the Bishop ordained William Vesey, who had been educated at Harvard, and who, before making the trip to England, had served as a lay reader at Hempstead. On his return to New York, Vesey served first as an assistant minister and then was inducted as rector on Christmas Day, 1697, beginning a period of service that was exercised under the administration of ten royal governors until his death in 1746. Vesey's integrity and moderation during his long ministry did much to reconcile all but the most determined Dissenters to the presence of the Church in the colony.

An Act of Establishment had been passed in 1693, which provided that 'a sufficient Protestant minister' should be settled in New York County and Richmond County (Staten Island), with two in each of the counties of Westchester and Queens.[2] Although the intention of the Assembly, which was then dominated by the Dutch and the Dissenters, has long been disputed, it is significant that no such provision was made for Suffolk County, where the Independents were strongest, or for Kings, Dutchess, Orange, and Albany Counties, which were strongholds of the Dutch, and that in English usage the phrase 'sufficient Protestant minister' meant a clergyman of the Church of England.

The parishes, of course, were to be supported by the payment of ecclesiastical taxes and during the early years of settlement were supplied by missionary priests who were sent out by the S.P.G., from which they received regular stipends. During the period there was a very considerable shifting of these missionaries between posts in New York and neighboring New England. By 1729 there were churches at New Rochelle, Eastchester, and Rye. While the course of events in Westchester County was by no means an even one, on Long Island opposition to Anglicanism was the strongest and the dispute stormiest. In Jamaica in 1710 the Dissenters seized church and rectory and called a Dissenting minister, refusing to pay the minister sent by the Society. The missionary brought suit for his salary and won, but the church was awarded to the Presbyterians in a decision worthy of Solomon, and the Episcopalians found it necessary to build another church. At Hempstead, where the other minister in Queens County was located, opposition was briefer and less severe, and by 1719 some of the residents of Suffolk County had applied to the S.P.G. for a minister. They eventually built up a thriving parish at Setauket, where the first missionary, James Wetmore, one of the Yale converts, arrived late in 1723. Caroline Church, which is still standing, was built six years later by his successor (plate 70). On Staten Island a church and parsonage were built and a glebe was purchased by 1715, entirely through voluntary subscriptions.[3] Although no provision was made for Albany County, as early as 1709 an S.P.G. missionary was sent there, who also received an allowance from the British government for his services to the soldiers at that frontier post. A missionary was later also maintained at the Mohawk Castle to work among the Indians. A number of the Hudson Valley patroon families appear to have rather readily embraced the Church of England, and missionary work began in Dutchess County in the 1750's.[4] In 1769, Trinity Church, which is still extant, was built at Fishkill.

In 1709 Trinity Parish, in the City of New York, was the recipient of a gift of land for its endowment, known as the Queen's Farm and consisting of about 62 acres near the churchyard in lower Manhattan. This valuable property enabled Trinity Parish in later years to assume its unique roll in assisting various worthy religious and civic enterprises and in maintaining other parishes as well as itself during the difficult years immediately after the abolition of the Establishment. As early as 1709 Trinity had established a charity school, and in 1752 it opened St. George's Chapel, which became an independent parish in 1811. King's College, now Columbia University, was founded in 1754 largely by Trinity Church, which gave the block of ground on which its first building was erected.[5] Under conditions of the gift, the Book of Common Prayer was always to be used in the chapel.

The first president was Dr. Samuel Johnson, another of the Yale converts and by this time one of the most learned of the colonial clergy, who also served as assistant minister and lecturer at Trinity Church.[6] After the Revolution the Right Reverend Dr. Benjamin Moore, who was rector of Trinity and second bishop of New York at the same time, served as president of the college.

The establishment of the Church in New York is a rather complex story differing greatly from county to county. Its founding and growth in Pennsylvania and the counties that are now Delaware is somewhat simpler. From the start, religious toleration was provided in William Penn's colony, although freedom of worship for members of the Church of England was specially ensured by a clause in the proprietary charter of 1681. The Reverend John Yeo had already come to New Castle from Maryland as early as 1677 and held services in the Delaware settlements for some years, but had returned to Maryland by 1682.[7] It was not until 1695 that Christ Church was founded in Philadelphia by a group of thirty-six Church of England laymen in that city. The first clergyman sent out to the parish was the Reverend Thomas Clayton, who lived for only two years and was succeeded by the Reverend Evan Evans, who soundly planted the Church in Pennsylvania during a ministry of eighteen years. Evans was supported by local contributions plus a stipend of £50 from the S.P.G. and soon obtained the services of an assistant. He also preached in other communities near Philadelphia, and is claimed to have held services in Welsh among the people who founded St. David's, Radnor (plate 69).

During the eighteenth century, following the conversion to Anglicanism of George Keith, an influential orthodox Quaker, and his assumption of a mission under the S.P.G., an increasing number of Quakers, including the proprietors, went over to the English Church. By the early 'sixties the congregation of Christ Church had become so large that a second congregation, St. Peter's, was established by the vestry of Christ Church, on an equal footing with the mother church, to be governed by a vestry and served by the same ministers. This was a compromise arrangement. A new parish was not created as was the practice in Boston. Neither was the new congregation maintained as a chapel of the principal church, as in New York.

About the same time St. Paul's Church was organized by a Whitefieldian wing of the congregation of Christ Church Parish. In 1755 the College of Philadelphia (now the University of Pennsylvania) had been organized under the sponsorship of Benjamin Franklin and the Reverend William Smith, its first provost and one of the most able of the provincial clergy. It was probably owing to the influence of Dr. Smith that the Venerable Society agreed to move into the Pennsylvania frontier and to send a missionary into York and Cumberland Counties in 1758.[8]

Regular missions were established at New Castle in 1704, at Dover in 1705, and at Lewes in 1722. One had been established at Appoquinimy (now Middletown, Delaware) in 1708, which was left vacant for years after the brief stay of the Reverend Thomas Jenkins, who had been sent to New Castle County by the S.P.G. at that time. Contemporary conditions in the lower counties are reflected in the letter the Reverend John Talbot wrote to the S.P.G. on 27 September 1709. In it he stated that, 'Poor Brother Jenkins at Appoquinimy was baited to death by Musquitoes and blood thirsty Gal Knippers, which would not let him rest night nor day. till he got a fever, came to Philadelphia and died immediately. These places must be served by itinerants and it is hardly possible for anybody to abide there, that is not born there, till he is musquito proof.'[9]

Delaware is almost as closely linked with neighboring New Jersey in its early ecclesiastical history as it is with Pennsylvania. The Reverend John Talbot arrived in New Jersey with the newly ordained Reverend George Keith, in 1703, as the first missionaries sent to the American continent by the S.P.G. Both preached in New Jersey, but Talbot settled at Burlington, where he continued to serve until his dismissal by the S.P.G. several years before his death. He had labored tirelessly for years whenever he could assist the Church elsewhere in the area, and was a leader in the movement to obtain a bishop for the Middle Colonies; but repeated accusations that he was a Jacobite, and rumors of his consecration as a bishop by the Non-Jurors during a visit to England brought about his replacement by Nathaniel Harwood in 1727. By 1724 six New Jersey parishes were listed in the records of the S.P.G., including those at Burlington, Elizabeth, Perth Amboy, and Salem.[10] In 1734 a missionary was sent to Monmouth, and although a church was organized at Newark about the same time, a resident clergyman was not appointed to that post until 1751.

The clergy who served these Middle Colonies appear to have been relatively diligent in reading Morning and Evening Prayer, in catechizing the youth, and in holding monthly celebrations of the Holy Communion. Indeed Talbot in 1724 stated that he read Morning and Evening Prayer in his church each day, and thought that he was the only minister in America who did so.[11] In this connection it may be stated that most of the clergymen in New York and New Jersey were High Churchmen, while those in

Pennsylvania were Latitudinarian in their views, though at the same time they maintained a high standard of church life in comparison to the Virginia clergy. In contrast to the relatively generous income which some Maryland priests received, the average income in New Jersey in 1724 was £60 per year from the Society plus £20 to £30 from the parish.[12]

One unique feature of the Church's development in the Middle Colonies must be mentioned. The Swedes had been the first settlers along the Delaware River and had erected a number of churches in Pennsylvania, Delaware, and New Jersey. Relations between the Swedish Lutheran and Anglican clergy were always of the most cordial sort. The Swedish ministers joined in laying the cornerstones of new Anglican churches and occasionally filled pulpits whose occupants were absent, without the validity of their orders ever being questioned. One pastor, the Reverend Andreas Rudman, was appointed by the S.P.G. in 1705 as its minister at Oxford, Pennsylvania. Although there had been a gradual trend in that direction, at the end of the War of Independence most congregations voted to transfer their allegiance to the New Protestant Episcopal Church in the United States. Early buildings erected by Swedish congregations still exist in Philadelphia (Gloria Dei; plate 65), in Wilmington (Holy Trinity; plate 66), and at Swedesboro (Trinity; plate 93).

When the Revolution came, all but one minister in New Jersey, Robert Blackwell at Gloucester, closed their churches, but although many fled, four remained in the colony to open their churches again in 1782 when the war seemed near an end. In New York, where, except for the first year after the opening of hostilities, the city was occupied by the British forces, the churches were able to carry on much as usual. The Reverend Charles Inglis, rector of Trinity Parish, left with the British troops after the Treaty of 1783 and became the first bishop of Nova Scotia. The Reverend Samuel Provoost, an ardent Patriot, who had been an assistant at Trinity but had resigned in 1769 and who had served with the American forces during the war, returned to become rector and subsequently first bishop of New York. Provoost was active in making regular visitations for Confirmation and consecrated a number of new churches in the state. On his retirement in 1801 he was succeeded by Benjamin Moore, who had been a Loyalist and had faithfully served as an assistant minister both during and since the Revolution. Under his leadership the Church began the continuous growth which was so spectacularly extended under Hobart, his great successor.

In Pennsylvania, only the Reverend William White, who became rector of Christ Church, Philadelphia, during the Revolution, remained at his post throughout most of the period; at one time he was the only Episcopal minister in the state.[13] A man of great ability, a sincere Patriot, son of a wealthy family, and brother-in-law of Robert Morris, financier of the Revolution, he was at the same time sufficiently moderate in his views to have the confidence of his fellow clergymen, on both Whig and Tory sides. It was White's destiny to exercise the central leadership, aided by William Smith of Maryland, former provost of the College of Philadelphia, which finally brought about the reorganization of the Church in the United States.

As already indicated, the architectural characteristics of the churches in the Middle Colonies, like the social and political qualities of the region, partook of the extremes that typified their neighbors to the north and south, tempered, however, by local conditions. As a result it is more difficult to segregate distinctive architectural types and attributes. Perhaps the best that can be done is to emphasize the more obvious groupings or types of ecclesiastical structures built in the several states of the Middle Atlantic region and point out their similarities and kinship to prototypes in the South and in New England.

In the Middle Colonies, as elsewhere in English North America, the first churches were primitive wooden buildings, which have largely disappeared and have been replaced by more ambitious ones built in more permanent fashion. An excellent example of this early type of church still exists, however, in Christ Church, Broad Creek Hundred, Delaware (plates 91–2). Although the church was not built until 1771, the parish was located in a relatively remote quarter that was long under dispute with Maryland. The exterior and interior of the walls are roughly finished in wooden sheathing and all furniture and trim is not only of the simplest sort but has remained unpainted. The Church at Dagsboro, Delaware, is also of frame construction.

The other English churches in the lower counties are of brick. Most of them were built to succeed the more humble early buildings and, while they appear to have been much influenced by the parish churches of neighboring Maryland, it must be remembered that they were built through voluntary subscriptions and received no support from taxation. Thus they are relatively small, with simple brickwork and usually a barrel-vaulted ceiling. They are properly oriented with the chancel at the east end and the pulpit and reading desk in the center of the north wall. The galleries varied with the requirements of the congregation and the location of the high pulpit. Thus, that at Broad Creek Hundred is in the west end, while at Appoquinimy and Dover the galleries were on both the west and south walls, and at Dagsboro and Indian River Hundred they were on three sides. The trim and the furniture of these Delaware churches were very simple and in none of them are there any surviving tablets of the Law, nor are any references to these customary decorations known.[14]

The beautiful and relatively elaborate church at New Castle in its present form is the result of several enlargements. During the last, in 1820, the church was reoriented and the tower, steeple, and transepts were added. Originally it was a typical simple rectangular brick structure 50 feet long by 30 feet wide and was no doubt influenced by Holy Trinity, built by the Swedes at Wilmington in 1699. Each of these rectangular buildings was built in three bays with arched windows and a jerkin-head roof, and in the case of both structures, porches were added at an early date to support the weak longitudinal walls.[15] St. Anne's, Appoquinimy (1768), perhaps the finest of the Delaware churches, is a departure from the usual pattern. It is built in five bays with two tiers of windows. The walls are laid up in Flemish bond with glazed headers accented by a pleasing cove cornice. The pedimented gables and the large Palladian window, which pierces the east wall, suggest that the design of the church may have been inspired by St. Peter's in Philadelphia, completed seven years earlier (plates 78, 90).

The smaller parish churches in Pennsylvania were originally of the same simple, rectangular form that prevailed in Delaware and was popular in Maryland. In their original form Trinity Church, Oxford (1711), and St. David's, Radnor (1715), were excellent examples. Both were once small rectangular buildings in which the pulpit probably was placed across from the side door, while the chancel occupied the end wall. The former structure was altered by the addition of transepts and tower and by the blocking of the north door during the first half of the nineteenth century. The church is built of brick, laid in Flemish bond with glazed headers, while tiny St. David's is built of fieldstone. Fortunately the latter retains much of its original appearance (plate 69).

It is in the metropolitan churches of the old city of Philadelphia that Pennsylvania's greatest ecclesiastical architectural interest lies. Gloria Dei, built by the Swedes in 1698, bespeaks her special heritage (plate 65). In the others the distinct Philadelphia flavor is rather subtly compounded. It is derived partly from the superb quality of interior ornaments, fashioned by the same cabinetmakers who made Philadelphia pieces in the Chippendale style one of the great glories of eighteenth-century American furniture. In part it comes from fine craftsmanship in brick and stone, and the somewhat sober and rather heavy elegance that characterized the taste of the wealthy merchants who set the cultural tone of the colonial city. Christ Church (1727) is a large rectangular auditory church with a tower and spire in the general style popularized by Wren. The heavy, rather baroque quality of its brick and stone exterior ornamentation presents an interesting—almost Carolinian—contrast to the New England severity of its contemporary structure, Christ Church in Boston (plates 71, 100). St. Peter's (1758) is an interesting Georgian building 90 by 60 feet in dimensions, with a tower that originally supported a low cupola. The tower was extended and crowned with the present spire by Strickland early in the nineteenth century. He was responsible for less happy alterations to the simpler St. Paul's Church.

It is in New York and New Jersey that it is most difficult to find any definite architectural pattern among the early churches, although one definite distinction exists in the frequent use of the native brown stone as a lasting material for these buildings. In both states there are numerous white clapboard churches that are reminiscent of New England, while the brick churches found in New Jersey, at least in their original form, were most closely allied to similar structures in Pennsylvania and Delaware.

Notable stone examples exist in St. George's, Schenectady (1769), an irregular cruciform structure with hipped roof, tower, and steeple, and in St. Paul's, Eastchester (1761; plate 81). The latter, built with five bays of tall arched windows, has an unusual feature in its brick window trim. Christ Church, New Brunswick, New Jersey (1743), and St. Thomas', Alexandria, New Jersey (1769), are other interesting stone edifices. The best stone church is, of course, St. Paul's Chapel, New York. Lineal descendant of the first Trinity Parish Church of 1698, which was destroyed by fire in 1776, it might well be termed the finest of the early structures considered in these pages. Accented by rather heavy Mid-Georgian detail, its exterior nevertheless attains a soaring grace that is achieved among the larger contemporary American buildings by only a few of the best wooden meeting-houses of New England.

The wooden buildings in New York and New Jersey that are still standing bear a decided family resemblance to the earlier New England churches. Both Caroline Church, Setauket, Long Island (1729), and Christ Church, Shrewsbury (1769), are shingled and both are alike in retaining British emblems atop their spires—a Union Jack in the weathervane at Caroline Church and a crown at Shrewsbury (plate 70). (A similar finial tops Trinity's spire in Newport.) Trinity Church, Fishkill (1769), and Christ Church, Duanesburg (1789), on the other hand, are sided with narrow weatherboards and are rather reminiscent of St. Paul's Church at Wickford, Rhode Island—an early structure of conventional meeting-house type. It is as difficult, however, to establish any particular architectural pattern among the eighteenth-century frame churches in New York and New Jersey as it is among the limited number of brick structures. Old St. Mary's at Burlington, although first erected in 1703 as a small rectangular church similar to those in Delaware, was greatly altered and enlarged by Strickland and is today cruciform in plan and is finished in yellow stucco and Greek Revival trim. In contrast, Trinity Church, Swedesboro (1784), is included in the following photographs (plate 93) as a vigorously executed eighteenth-century brick edifice of late Georgian inspiration.

In general it may be said that New York and New Jersey churches were originally built on a rectangular plan—indeed this is true of contemporary church buildings in all of the states north of Maryland. Stone or wood was preferred as material, and in most cases there is a tower and spire, or a cupola or steeple, springing from the main fabric. Interior finish and furniture vary greatly although the embellishment of several New York structures is unusually opulent compared to that of colonial contemporaries elsewhere. For example, armorial tombstones are found in and around many early Episcopal churches, but few have heraldic mural monuments comparable to those found in New York. Eighteenth-century elegance in an American church reaches its peak in the interior of St. Paul's Chapel.

Episcopal Churches in the Middle States which were Erected

before 1808 and are still Standing:

DELAWARE

1698	Holy Trinity Church (Old Swede's)	Wilmington	New Castle County
1703	Immanuel Church	New Castle	New Castle County
1734	Christ Church	Dover	Kent County
1757	Prince George's Chapel	Dagsboro	Sussex County
1768	St. Anne's	Appoquinimy, Middletown	New Castle County
1771	Christ Church	Broad Creek Hundred, near Laurel	Sussex County
1794	St. George's Chapel	Indian River Hundred, near Angola	Sussex County

PENNSYLVANIA

1697	Gloria Dei	Philadelphia	Philadelphia County
1711	Trinity Church	Oxford	Philadelphia County
1715	St. David's Church	Radnor	Delaware County
1727	Christ Church	Philadelphia	Philadelphia County
1745	St. Peter's in the Great Valley	East Whiteland	Chester County
1758	St. Peter's Church	Philadelphia	Philadelphia County
1760	Christ Church	Bridgeport	Montgomery County
1760	St. James' Church	Kingsessing	Philadelphia County
1761	St. Paul's Church	Philadelphia	Philadelphia County
1766	St. John's Church	York	York County
1785	St. James' Church	Perkiomen	Montgomery County
1785	St. James' Church	Bristol	Bucks County
1786	St. John's Church	Concord	Delaware County

NEW JERSEY

1703	Old St. Mary's Church	Burlington	Burlington County
1733	St. Peter's Church	Freehold	Monmouth County

1743	Christ Church (tower original, nave rebuilt in 1852)	New Brunswick	Middlesex County
1748	St. Michael's Church (rebuilt in 1819)	Trenton	Mercer County
1769	Christ Church	Shrewsbury	Monmouth County
1769	St. Thomas' Church	Alexandria	Hunterdon County
1784	Trinity Church	Swedesboro	Gloucester County
1786	Zion Church (originally Moravian)	Sharptown	Salem County

NEW YORK

1729	Caroline Church	Setauket	Suffolk County
1735	St. James' Chapel	Elmhurst	Queens County
1752	St. John's Church (rebuilt 1870)	Tuckahoe	Westchester County
1761	St. Paul's Church, Eastchester	Mt. Vernon	Westchester County
1764	St. Paul's Chapel	New York	Borough of Manhattan
1765	St. John's Church	Oakdale	Suffolk County
1767	St. Peter's Church	Van Cortlandtville	Westchester County
1769	St. George's Church	Schenectady	Schenectady County
1769	Trinity Church	Fishkill	Dutchess County
1789	Christ Church	Duanesburg	Schenectady County
1795	St. Mark's Church	New York	Borough of Manhattan
1803	St. Luke's Church	Richfield	Otsego County
1803	St. Paul's Church	Charlton	Saratoga County
1807	Trinity Church	Fairfield	Herkimer County

65. Gloria Dei, Philadelphia, Pennsylvania, 1697

On 19 September 1697, ground was broken for a new Swedish church on the Delaware River. Now in the industrial heart of Philadelphia, its Swedish architectural heritage is unmistakable. The building was dedicated by its first pastor, the Reverend Eric Bjork, on 2 July 1700, as Gloria Dei, to commemorate the gratitude of the fifty-seven Swedish families who comprised its first congregation. In 1710 permission was given to members of the Church of England to worship in Gloria Dei after the Swedish service each Sunday. At the later service a hymn was always sung in Swedish as a token of the harmony between both groups. Eventually the English congregation far outnumbered the Swedes and the church became a regular parish of the Protestant Episcopal Church.

66. *Holy Trinity Church, Wilmington, Delaware, 1698*

The granite walls of Holy Trinity were built by the Swedish settlers who had been in Delaware since 1638. Their second church at Christina settlement, now Wilmington, was dedicated on Trinity Sunday of the year 1699. The English population increased rapidly, and by 1742, under Pastor Tranberg, it was decided that while the morning service should continue to be held in Swedish, the afternoon service should be conducted in English. In 1792 the church was served by its first regular rector in Anglican orders, the Reverend Joseph Clarkson.

The steep A-truss of the roof spread the stone walls, despite their thickness, and the south porch was added in 1750 to counteract this. A gallery with twenty-five additional pews was added in 1774. It was reached by the delightful exterior staircase within the south porch. The west tower and belfry were added in 1802.

The interior is of great simplicity with brick-paved aisles and chancel, the original pulpit with its flat sounding board, and heavy doors accented by great wrought-iron hinges and fittings. The silver communion cup, paten, and wafer box sent out from Sweden to the parish in 1718 are still in use.

67. *Old St. Mary's Church, Burlington, New Jersey,* 1703

Although the nave was erected in 1703, the fact would never be recognized from either the exterior or the interior of this venerable building. The church was enlarged three times, in 1769, 1810, and again by William Strickland in 1834. His enthusiasm for the classic Greek style resulted in the over-all application of stucco to the old pink brick and the use of appropriate trim. Wings were also added to the north and south sides, bringing the rectangular building to the form of a Greek cross.

The cornerstone was laid by the Reverend John Talbot, and his friend, the Reverend George Keith, preached the first sermon heard in the church on 22 August 1703. They were the first of the great company of missionaries sent to America by the Society for the Propagation of the Gospel. It was at Burlington that the clergy of New York, New Jersey, and Pennsylvania, joined by the Swedish pastors Bjork and Rudman, met on 2 November 1705 and drafted a letter to the archbishops and the S.P.G. asking for the appointment of a suffragan bishop for the North American colonies.

68. *Immanuel Church, New Castle, Delaware, 1703*

High above one of the most charming old towns in North America rises the spire of Immanuel. Its nave is the brick building that had almost been completed when the Reverend George Ross arrived in New Castle in 1705, as its first regular Anglican priest. His parishioners had placed it on the village green, he explained in a letter to England, 'from a persuasion that, as it belonged to their sovereign, it was not in the power of any of their troublesome neighbors to disturb them.' The chancel was changed from the east to the west end of the church when William Strickland enlarged and redesigned the rectangular building in 1820, adding the transepts, tower, and steeple.

STEPHEN P. DORSEY

EARLY CHURCHES IN THE MIDDLE STATES · 125

69. *St. David's Church, Radnor, Pennsylvania, 1715*

St. David's was built in 1715 in fulfillment of a promise made by the Welsh settlers that they would build a stone church for their missionary, the Reverend John Clubb. This fine little structure, only 40 feet in length, is distinguished by the robust architectural quality of its masonry and woodwork.

Here every fortnight the Reverend Evan Evans, second rector of Christ Church, Philadelphia, preached in Welsh to those who lived in what was then known as the Welsh Baronetcy. After the resignation of its Loyalist rector at the outbreak of the Revolution, no services were held in St. David's for the duration of the war, though both Continental and British troops used the premises for various purposes. After the battle of Brandywine, sixteen British soldiers were interred in the churchyard and here lies the body of 'Mad Anthony' Wayne, the Continental General.

70. *Caroline Church of Brookhaven, Setauket, Long Island, New York,* 1729

Caroline Church, originally Christ Church, was renamed in 1730 after the gift of a silver communion service and embroidered altar cloths by Queen Caroline, the consort of George II. It was the first Anglican church organized in Suffolk County, which was predominantly nonconformist in its sympathies. The first minister to serve the congregation was the Reverend James Wetmore, one of the Yale converts, who spent a brief time at Setauket in the winter of 1723–4. From 1814 until 1844 its rector was the Reverend Charles Seabury, son of the first American bishop.

Except for the warped walls, the exterior is much as it was originally, and the weathervane still embodies the first Union Jack. The structural timbers are of hand-hewn oak while the floors are of pine boards, some of which are sixteen inches wide. The barrel-vaulted interior has a gallery at the rear.

GEORGE C. CALDER

71. *Christ Church, Philadelphia, Pennsylvania,* 1727

Christ Church was founded 15 November 1695 by thirty-six laymen, among whom were a judge of the Admiralty, the Attorney General, physicians, lawyers, sea captains, merchants, carpenters, a dyer, a baker, and two men supposed to have been pirates.

The present Georgian building, reminiscent of Wren's London churches, was begun in 1727 at the west end, as an enlargement of the old church. The next decade saw the replacement of the eastern two-thirds of the old building by the present fabric, which was completed in 1744. The steeple, which was later topped by a great gilded miter, was added in 1754. Within the tower hangs a peal of eight bells cast by the Whitechapel Bell Foundry and brought from England in that same year.

Dr. Kearsley is generally credited as the architect, but he may only have been in charge of the work, designed by someone unknown. The names of Robert Smith and 'Mr. Harrison,' both of the Carpenters' Company, are connected with the steeple, which was based on 'the draft which Mr. Harrison drew.' Construction was directed by Robert Smith.

This first Anglican church in the colony became the mother of many churches in the city and elsewhere in Pennsylvania. Four-fifths of the first Board of Trustees of the University of Pennsylvania, founded in 1740 by Benjamin Franklin, were men of Christ Church. Here on 7 July 1775, members of Congress heard the rector preach on 'The Duty of Standing Fast in our Spiritual and Temporal Liberties.' George Washington was a member of the congregation from 1790 to 1797. Among other notable pew holders were John Penn, the last provincial governor, Benjamin Franklin, Robert Morris, John Adams, and Betsy Ross.

The first General Convention met at Christ Church in 1785, and here at the Convention of 1789 the organization of the Protestant Episcopal Church was completed and the first American House of Bishops met.

PHILIP B. WALLACE

PHILIP B. WALLACE

72. *The Chancel—Christ Church, Philadelphia*

The present altar encloses the holy table presented in 1789. A communion service presented by Queen Anne in 1708, which was used when members of the Continental Congress gave thanks after the battle of Yorktown, is still employed for special celebrations.

Beyond the reading desk may be seen the brass marking the tomb of Bishop White. Under the tablet bearing the Ten Commandments is a mural monument to Brigadier General Forbes, 'Colonel of the 17th Reg't of Foot and Commander of His Majesty's Troops in the Southern Provinces of North America,' who was interred beneath the chancel in 1759. The interior is relatively sumptuous as might be expected of what was once the most elaborate church in the greatest city of the American colonies.

PHILIP B. WALLACE

73. *The Cathedra—Christ Church*

The first Episcopal chair known to have been made for this purpose in America was presented by John Swanwick on 11 October 1787, to the Rt. Reverend William White, D.D., first bishop of the diocese of Pennsylvania and first chaplain of the Continental Congress. Bishop White also served as rector of Christ Church for fifty-seven years until his death, 17 July 1836.

PHILIP B. WALLACE

74. *The Pulpit—Christ Church, Philadelphia*

The white and gold wine-glass pulpit, which originally stood at the end of the middle alley, was made by John Folwell in 1770.

75. *The Organ—Christ Church, Philadelphia*

The present organ has been fitted to the case which enclosed the old Ludovic Spragel organ of 1765. In the tower room beyond is the library founded in 1696 containing the service books from which all references to the king were struck out on 4 July 1776.

76 AND 77. *Philadelphia Fonts*

Philadelphia should be as well known for its church furniture as for the superb domestic furniture it produced in the eighteenth century. The Christ Church font, on the left, was brought from England in 1697. Although it is extremely simple, it contains a massive silver bowl of sixty-three ounces, given in 1712. While not as elaborate as that at St. Peter's, the font on the right from St. Paul's Church (1761) is an excellent example of the Philadelphia cabinetmaker's art. It also holds a silver bowl, this one delicately fluted.

78. *St. Peter's Church, Philadelphia, Pennsylvania, 1758*

The restrained classic exterior detail of St. Peter's is in marked contrast to the baroque characteristics of nearby Christ Church, to which it had originally been attached as a chapel of ease. The interior of the church is airy and spacious and as beautifully preserved as the exterior—all of the original box pews remain as they were in the eighteenth century. Among the monuments in the crowded churchyard is that of Commodore Stephen Decatur, the naval hero, who was killed in a duel at Bladensburg outside of Washington in 1820. One gravestone is dated 1760, a year before the building was opened.

PHILIP B. WALLACE

79. *The Pulpit and Reading Desk—St. Peter's, Philadelphia*

The high pulpit, reached by a stairway within the wall, is unique. It stands opposite the altar at the west end of the main alley.

80. *The Chancel and Organ—St. Peter's, Philadelphia*

The organ, first installed in the north gallery in 1764, was set up over the chancel in 1789. In 1782 a committee was appointed to regulate the singing at St. Peter's and to make arrangements for the instruction of a choir of twelve persons. The vase-type font of highly polished mahogany, which is placed within the chancel, is among the finest in any American colonial church. It is carved with a dove, cherubs' heads, and foliage. The chancel chairs resemble the cathedra at Christ Church.

WILLIAM C. FAUST

81. *St. Paul's Church, Eastchester, New York, 1761*

Unusual features of this imposing church are its steeple and the use of gauged brick trim with stone walls. It has a single tier of tall arched windows in five bays with a door in the center of the north wall opposite the pulpit. Over the pulpit on the south wall are placed tablets of the Decalogue. The chancel occupies a smaller extension with two bays of arched windows and a great circular window in its east gable. The church stands on the old village green, which was a general training ground and election place during colonial times. It was temporarily used as a military hospital during the American Revolution and was briefly converted into a courthouse during the year 1787.

STEPHEN P. DORSEY

82. *St. Paul's Chapel, The Parish of Trinity Church in the City of New York*, 1764

Dwarfed by near-by skyscrapers, and soot-blackened as it is, St. Paul's may be considered the finest Georgian ecclesiastical structure in America—not only for the richness of its original appointments, but by reason of its superb scale, proportions, and ornamental detail. It is the oldest public building on Manhattan Island in its original state, and is reminiscent of Gibbs' St. Martin's-in-the-Fields built in 1720. The body of the church was completed in 1766 of native stone, 'Manhattan mica-schist,' with quoins and trim of brownstone from designs by Thomas McBean, a Scot who is said to have studied under Gibbs. The portico and spire were added in 1794-6, perhaps under the direction of L'Enfant.

Ten years later, this chapel of Trinity Parish, in what were then the suburbs, was spared by the great fire that destroyed the first Trinity Church. The structure of 7 bays is 112 feet in length, and its exquisite spire soars to a height of 219 feet. Above the Broadway portico is a heroic statue of St. Paul, carved from oak, according to tradition, by the sculptor of the first figurehead of the United States Frigate *Constitution;* beneath it, directly behind the altarpiece, is the monument to Major General Richard Montgomery, who fell in the attack on Quebec, 31 December 1775.

During the period of the British occupation of New York, St. Paul's served as the military chapel of the commander. Here worshiped the sailor prince, Prince William (afterward William IV), Lord Cornwallis, Sir Guy Carleton, Lord Howe, and Major André. Many British officers are buried in the churchyard as are four of Washington's officers, who were original members of the Cincinnati, and the Sieur de Rochefontaine, one of his French allies.

On 30 April 1789, immediately following his inauguration, the first President with his entire official family attended a Service of Thanksgiving at St. Paul's and continued to worship there for several years. Washington's pew is on the north aisle. Above it are the arms of the United States and in it stand the headquarters flag and colors of the Continental Army. The arms of the State of New York hang over Governor Clinton's pew on the south aisle.

St. Paul's is more than an American Revolutionary shrine. In view of its early connection with the Loyalist Americans and the British in New York, many services of memory or thanksgiving have been held through the years on days of special significance to the British Empire. Thus it has continued to serve as a concrete bond between the two great English-speaking peoples.

FRANK CLEVELAND

83. *The Pulpit—St. Paul's Chapel*

The exquisitely carved pulpit of white and gold carries out the theme of the altarpiece and chancel fittings. The three feathers of the Prince of Wales' crest still surmount the tester or sounding board.

84. *View of the Chancel from the Nave—St. Paul's Chapel*

Above the center alley may be seen several of the fourteen original Waterford cut-glass chandeliers which hang from a ceiling of cerulean blue. The organ in the rear gallery is contained in the original organ case of 1802.

FRANK CLEVELAND

COURTESY PARISH OF TRINITY CHURCH IN THE CITY OF NEW YORK

86. *St. Paul's Chapel*

85. *The High Altar—St. Paul's Chapel*

The first mausoleum-type altar known to have been built in an Anglican Church in America, with the baroque 'glory' above it, was designed about 1788 by Pierre Charles L'Enfant, Major of Engineers in the Continental Army, who afterwards drew the plans for the new city of Washington. The glory, which reflects the French baroque heritage of L'Enfant, represents Mount Sinai in clouds and lightning, the tables of the Law, and the Hebrew characters for Jehovah in the triangle—symbolizing the Deity and the continuity of the Church of the Old and the New Testaments. In the chancel are four walnut chairs, *c*.1690, believed to be part of the furniture of the first Trinity Church.

87. *Memorial Tablets in Chancel—St. Paul's Chapel*

To the rear of the pulpit in the chancel may be seen the mural monument embellished with the arms of Sir John Temple, Bart., first British Consul General to the United States of America, appointed after the Revolution. He died 17 November 1798 and is interred beneath the chancel. Similar memorial wall tablets are placed here to the memory of Colonel Thomas Barclay, son of the second rector of Trinity Parish and British Consul General to the United States from 1799 to 1830; to Margaret Inglis, wife of the last colonial rector of Trinity who became first bishop of Nova Scotia; and to Elizabeth Franklin, wife of the royal governor of New Jersey and daughter-in-law of Benjamin Franklin.

COURTESY LIBRARY OF CONGRESS

88. *Sentence of Consecration of the Second Trinity Church*

Signed by Samuel Provoost, Bishop of New York, 25 March 1790

89. *The Second Trinity Church in* 1789

From a contemporary woodcut. This structure had a strong influence on the building of Gothic Revival churches in New England until it was razed in 1839.

90. St. Anne's Church, Appoquinimy, Middletown, Delaware, 1768

Distinguishing features of this fine Georgian church are its cove cornice, pedimented gables, and great Palladian window over the altar, which indicate that it may have been inspired by St. Peter's, Philadelphia, built only a few years earlier. The lower tier of its five bays of windows is protected by solid wooden shutters. The brickwork is laid in Flemish bond with glazed headers. Within, the box pews of the nave are painted, while those of the L-shaped gallery on the west and south walls are unfinished. The pulpit originally stood at the middle of the north wall but was moved to the front of the church.

91. *Christ Church, Broad Creek Hundred, near Laurel, Delaware,* 1771

This primitive structure is a marked contrast to the sophisticated city churches on the immediately preceding pages. Christ Church was built in 1771 on the shore of Chipman's Pond—on land that until 1775 was claimed as part of Stepney Parish, Somerset County, Maryland. The unique beauty of this little Georgian chapel of ease among the pines lies in its primitive honesty and simplicity. Today it remains unaltered in almost as perfect condition as when it was completed by Robert Holton in 1772 at a cost of £510. Inside the church the rich brown patina of unpainted pine woodwork illumined by tall, arched, many-paned windows is as striking as the fragrance of the wood, which one notices as the doors are opened. Walls, box pews, barrel-vaulted ceiling—all the interior woodwork—are of the same resinous, fine-grained, broad, heart pine as the outside sheathing.

92. *Pulpit—Christ Church, Broad Creek*

The pulpit and reading desk, with crude, scroll saw ornamentation occupy the center of the north wall as they did in all of the early Delaware churches of the period. A gallery is placed in the west end opposite the chancel.

93. *Trinity Church, Swedesboro, New Jersey, 1784*

Over the entrance of this sturdy church a slab, set in the wall, bears the date when it was built by the Swedes who inhabited the region before the War of Independence. The building stands on a bluff at the intersection of the King's Highway and Raccoon Creek, with its spire rising high above the grove of maples, cedars, and buttonwoods that surrounds it. The doors are deeply recessed with heavy Georgian pediments. The congregation united with the Protestant Episcopal Church in the United States in 1789, five years after the building was erected. The old Swedish altar plate of 1730 is still used.

94. *Interior—Christ Church, Duanesburg, New York, 1789*

Twenty-two miles west of Albany is a plain white clapboard country church, built by James Duane, statesman, churchman, and land speculator. Around it he planned to promote a settlement that would eclipse Schenectady, but today it is surrounded by only a few old houses. Except for the oil lamps and stovepipes the interior is virtually as it was when Duane and his family occupied the left front pew.

The simple interior paneling is in direct contrast to the painted heraldic embellishments of the marble tablets placed on the walls to the memory of members of the Duane family. That of the Honorable James Duane, member of the Continental Congress, a drafter of the Articles of Confederation, mayor of Manhattan from 1784 to 1789, and builder of the church, is placed at the left of the altar.

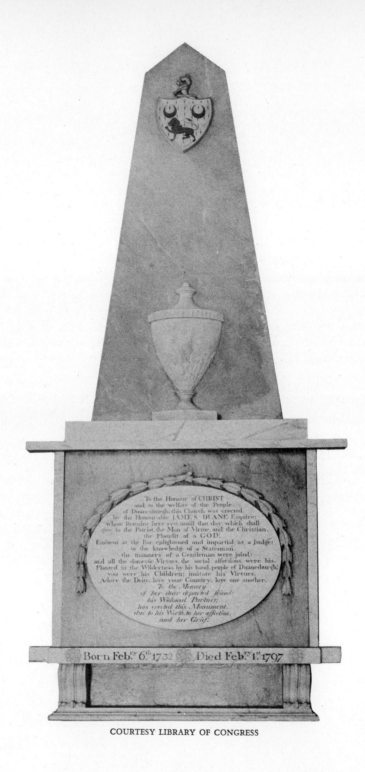

To the Honour of CHRIST
and to the welfare of the People
of Duanesburgh this Church was erected
by the Honourable JAMES DUANE Esquire:
whose Remains here rest, untill that day, which shall
give to the Patriot, the Man of Virtue, and the Christian,
the Plaudit of a GOD.
Eminent at the Bar, enlightened and impartial as a Judge:
to the knowledge of a Statesman,
the manners of a Gentleman were joind:
and all the domestic Virtues, the social affections were his.
Planted in the Wilderness by his hand, people of Duanesburgh,
you were his Children; imitate his Virtues.
Adore the Deity, love your Country, love one another.
To the Memory
of her dear departed friend:
his Widowed Partner:
has erected this Monument,
due to his Worth, to her affection,
and her Grief.

Born Feb.ʸ 6.ᵗʰ 1732   Died Feb.ʸ 1.ˢᵗ 1797

95. *Mural Monument—Christ Church, Duanesburg*

VI

Early Episcopal Churches in New England

THE INTRODUCTION of Anglicanism into New England was far different from its carefully nurtured inception in the South, where it was eventually afforded official preference and support in all of the colonies. In New England, Independence, or Congregationalism, was the zealously guarded established order, and the Anglicans had to share the bitter cup of the others who were dissenters in the eyes of the Puritan theocracy. Yet while the Church of England in the South grew in wealth and total numbers, any impartial appraisal of it must acknowledge a certain slackening of vitality during the second half of the eighteenth century, which made the Church's recovery particularly painful after the heavy blows it had suffered in the War of Independence. In New England, on the other hand, despite the harsh and unrelenting Puritan opposition, the growth of the Church during the eighteenth century was steady. Not only was the Revolutionary setback less severe than in the South, but after it, the Episcopal Church took on tremendous vigor, particularly in Connecticut. An examination of the list of churches built before 1808 and still standing in New England will indicate that about half of them were erected between 1785 and 1807, in marked contrast to the South, where almost no new churches were built for decades and where it was rather an era of destruction and decay.

The founders of Massachusetts, regarding the Church of England as poisoned by the twin evils of 'popery and prelacy,' stood at the opposite pole from the leaders of the Southern colonies. At first there was a distinction between the earliest settlers at Plymouth, who as Brownists felt that they must espouse complete separation from the Church of England, and the more conservative Puritans who colonized Massachusetts Bay. While in England the latter had been willing to remain in communion with the Church, provided that over-zealous bishops did not enforce conformity to practices which they considered corrupt.

In the New World, free from the restraints of the home government, these distinctions proved so slight that they quickly disappeared. Both groups found the 'Congregational' form of government more congenial to their common Calvinistic theology. They had come to New England not to establish a refuge for those seeking religious freedom in its exact sense, but rather to found a commonwealth in which the Church might be duly established according to their own ideas of its original purity. The legal code was to agree as nearly as possible with that of the Old Testament, and the elect, who alone would form the Church membership, were to be protected by the magistrates from the heretical or the ungodly. This system was first established at Plymouth, then in Massachusetts Bay, and, with the exception of Rhode Island, in the rest of New England, where it functioned relatively successfully for the next hundred years.

The 'new Israel,' however, did not remain entirely undisturbed. Charges were brought by the Plymouth Colony against a number of individuals who persisted in using the Book of Common Prayer. Two prominent members of the Salem Colony, the brothers Browne, were sent home to England for such practices, and the Reverend Francis Bright of the Salem Church, feeling that separation had gone too far, moved first to Charlestown, where he found matters little better, and then returned to England. Samuel Maverick, one of the 'old planters' found in the neighborhood of Boston when the Winthrop colonists arrived, as a staunch adherent of the Church of England was forbidden to hold office and was forced to live under other severe civil restraints, while his neighbor, Thomas Walford, was banished to New Hampshire. All in all, it has been estimated that nearly a hundred colonists returned to England rather than live under enforced Independency, and it seems probable that a number of others might have preferred the Church of England had they not been too weak a minority to be heard for the time being.[1]

Although the first successful settlements in Maine and New Hampshire were made by churchmen who provided for the encouragement of the Church of England, its life was cut short by the expanding Puritan power, and it was not revived until well into the eighteenth century. Sir Ferdinando Gorges' and Captain John Mason's grant of 1622 extended from the Merrimack to the Sagadahoc River and as far into the interior as the Great Lakes and the St. Lawrence. Mason, a zealous churchman, at his death in 1638 bequeathed one thousand acres for the maintenance of a preacher.

In 1640 a parish was organized at Strawberry Bank, now Portsmouth, New Hampshire, with a glebe of fifty acres granted by the governor for its support. A church and rectory were built, but the Reverend Richard Gibson, the first incumbent, returned to England in 1642 after his prosecution before the Massachusetts General Court which claimed jurisdiction over some of the islands where he had been serving the fishermen. The provincial charter Gorges obtained for Maine in 1639 provided for the establishment of the Church of England, and the following year the Reverend Robert Jordan arrived to minister to the settlements at Scarboro, Saco, and Casco (now Portland).[2] A leader in the resistance against the attempts of Massachusetts to establish her authority over Maine, he remained after the successful prosecution of the Massachusetts campaign until his house was destroyed by the Indians during King Philip's War.

During this early period, the repeated efforts of the Stuart kings to introduce the Church into New England met with strong opposition or were simply ignored by the

Puritans. Charles I issued an order in 1634 to transfer the government of New England to a group including the Archbishop of Canterbury and the Bishop of London, with power over both civil and ecclesiastical affairs. Although it was sent to Boston, nothing came of it.[3] His subsequent attempts met with similar failure. After the Restoration, Charles II repeatedly ordered the Massachusetts authorities to submit to the services of the Established Church, even including toleration of the Quakers among his demands. As many times, the independent government of the province refused to yield. It was not until the end of his reign that the charters of the New England colonies were revoked and plans made to unite them with New York under a single governor seated at Boston.

In 1686 Joseph Dudley was named 'President' of the colonies of Massachusetts, New Hampshire, Maine, and New York. The ship bearing Dudley's commission to Boston carried Robert Ratcliffe, an Episcopally ordained clergyman, who later became the first rector of King's Chapel. On the Sunday after his arrival, Ratcliffe, arrayed in the hated surplice, read the services of the Church in a room of the Town-House, the only place allowed for the purpose by the Council for the next several months. On 15 June 1686, the parish was formally organized, wardens were elected, some church furnishings were ordered, and the minister's salary established at £50 per year in addition to anything which the Council might grant him—not a promising source of income.[4] There is little difficulty in sensing the bitter hatred which the services inspired among the majority of the colonists. Tradesmen and merchants were warned by their creditors to stay away from them, and Ratcliffe was denounced as a 'Priest of Baal.'[5]

It took the hard hand of Sir Edmund Andros to make effective headway against such opposition. Succeeding Dudley, he was appointed the first royal governor of Massachusetts, arriving in the colony in 1687. He immediately demanded the use of one of the Boston meeting-houses for Anglican services. When no co-operation was forthcoming, he forced his way into Old South Church and beginning on Easter, 1687, the liturgy of the Church of England was read in that building every Sunday between the morning and afternoon services of the regular congregation. In spite of the constant friction that inevitably resulted, double use of the structure continued until the first wooden King's Chapel was ready for occupancy early in 1689.

Before the building was finished, news of the landing in England of William, Prince of Orange, reached the colony and was the occasion for a revolt against the local royal government. Andros and other officers were jailed, and the new King's Chapel was badly damaged by the mob. However, the Royal Governor was restored by the new King, who became a relatively generous donor to the parish.

The S.P.G., which was greatly interested in New England as a missionary field, in 1706 announced that it was ready to assist any duly recommended Harvard graduate willing to come to England for Episcopal ordination.[6] Within a decade missionaries had been sent to Braintree, Newbury, and Marblehead. In 1722 real impetus was given to the movement when the Reverend Timothy Cutler, a leading Puritan clergyman and president of Yale College at New Haven, Daniel Brown, a tutor at Yale, Samuel Johnson, pastor at West Haven, and four other Connecticut ministers publicly questioned the validity of their Congregational ordinations. While some of the converts relented, Cutler, Brown, Johnson, and James Wetmore soon went to England. Brown died of smallpox, but the other three were ordained and Cutler received the degree of Doctor of Sacred Theology from both Oxford and Cambridge.[7]

A second parish had become badly needed in Boston and on its organization, Christ Church called Cutler to be its rector. As such, with his distinguished background, he became a leader of the Anglican cause in Massachusetts. Johnson served for many years at Stratford, Connecticut, and eventually became president of King's College (now Columbia University) in New York. Although the example of the 'Yale Converts' caused anger and dismay in Puritan ranks, it was followed by a flow of conversions to Anglicanism as the gradual breakdown of the local Puritanism occurred.[8] While the Church continued a rather steady expansion in Massachusetts, it was in Connecticut that it experienced its strongest growth, although its history in that colony does not begin until 1706 with the visits of the Reverend George Muirson, the Society's missionary at Rye, and Colonel Caleb Heathcote, Lord of the Manor of Scarsdale, patron of Trinity Church, New York, and one of the most influential men of his time in the colonies. In 1722 Stratford obtained its first regular minister with the aid of the Society, and by 1750 there were twenty-four Episcopal churches in Connecticut in contrast to less than twenty in all the rest of New England.[9]

It seems probable that the rapid growth of the Church in Connecticut was partly due to several special causes. As a result of the early appearance of sizable groups of Quakers and Baptists, the religious history of the colony was long characterized by dissension and a struggle for toleration in which Anglicans could also join. Moreover, the Connecticut brand of Puritanism was more severe than that of Massachusetts. Under the latter colony's Half-Way Covenant, those who were not full members of the Church were admitted to certain limited privileges, including that of having their children baptized. This concession was never made in Connecticut, and as a result there were many good people who were still not of the elect and who had no religious privileges other than those of hearing the sermon and helping to pay the preacher. In such ground the Anglican doctrine and its more democratic system of local church administration could not help but bear fruit. Then too, there seems to have been a greater immigration of Church of England families into Connecticut than to her sister colony to the north.

The struggle for religious liberty in both colonies followed a similar pattern. Although persons differing from the established Congregational Church might hold their own services, they still had to pay taxes for the support of the establishment and its hostile ministers. In 1727 the General Court passed legislation by which religious taxes paid by members of the Church of England should be turned over to a minister of that Church, but only if the members were close enough to attend his church conveniently.

In Massachusetts an act of 1728 prevented a person from traveling more than five miles on Sunday and obliged him to pay taxes for the support of the local Congregational minister if he lived more than five miles from his own church. The protests of the Anglicans were vigorous, but it was not until 1735 that it became possible for persons attending the Church of England to pay their taxes for the support of their own clergymen. In both states, Episcopalians who lived in areas not supplied with their own clergy were still subject to prosecution if they did not pay their tax for support of the Congregational Church; this difficulty was not removed until its disestablishment some years after the Revolution.[10]

Rhode Island stood somewhat by itself among the New England colonies, with seven-tenths of its population in 1710 estimated as either Baptists or Quakers. The first Anglican priest was sent to Newport by Bishop Compton in 1700, and another was supplied at Narragansett in 1707. After somewhat stormy beginnings, the Church of England assumed steady growth, and S.P.G. missionaries were assigned to Bristol in 1722 and to Providence two years later. The early Puritan suppression of the Church in Maine and New Hampshire has already been mentioned. However, in 1734 a parish was successfully organized at Portsmouth, and after 1741, when Benning Wentworth began his long career as governor of New Hampshire, the Church entered a period of expansion under his support. The first missionary was assigned by the Society to Maine in 1755, and by 1768 two were working in the colony, one at Falmouth (now Portland) and the other as an itinerant serving Georgetown, Harpswell, Brunswick, Pownal, and certain other villages near the mouth of the Kennebec.[11]

The New England clergy were in great part native colonials who had been converted from Puritanism and who, as such, were men of sufficient strength of character to espouse their beliefs openly before a general public that was strongly prejudiced against them. They were relatively well educated and at the same time really knew the people to whom they ministered. Moreover, as converts, they laid particular stress upon the distinctive practices and institutions of the faith they had made their own. The feasts of the Church were faithfully kept in New England, and the Holy Communion was generally celebrated once a month. The remuneration for their faithful services, except in Boston, Newport, and Cambridge, was generally poor—made up as it was from what their parishioners could give, supplemented by a small stipend from the S.P.G. One struggling missionary who served two congregations at Dedham and Stoughton, Massachusetts, from 1770 until 1773 never received more than £15 sterling per year from both, in addition to his grant from the Society.[12]

With the Revolution, most of the New England clergy, adamant in their loyalty to their 'oath of the King's Supremacy,' eventually fled to New York, which was held by the British from 1776 until the end of the War, or to Canada or England. Although a number of the laity favored the Revolution, by its end only four Church of England ministers were left in Massachussetts, one in New Hampshire, and none in Maine.[13] A number of the clergy suffered severe persecution or imprisonment, but in Connecticut the majority continued to hold the stubborn course of loyalty.[14] When the War of Independence came to a conclusion, the Church in Connecticut, as the principal heir of colonial High Churchmanship, sought to obtain its own bishop as a first step in the re-organization of a national Episcopal Church. Although other New England Episco-palians were more receptive to unity, they tended to stand apart until Bishop Seabury's orders were accepted as valid by the churchmen of the other states.

After the acceptance of Seabury's Scottish consecration at the session of the Convention of 1789, that body adjourned for sufficient time for the Bishop and the Connecticut delegation as well as those from Massachusetts and New Hampshire to join it. Edward Bass, consecrated in 1797, a year after Seabury's death, was succeeded in 1804 by Samuel Parker, the leader of the Church in Massachusetts, who died less than a year after his consecration. Thereafter, the eastern diocese was left without a bishop until 1811 when Alexander Griswold was consecrated. Under his moderate Evangelical leadership the Church in New England continued to consolidate and push forward from its earlier advances.

Early Episcopal church buildings in any of the several New England states may be considered and compared on a regional basis without finding any marked architectural differences within the region, as there were farther south. All the churches express a common New England architectural heritage and, with only a few urban exceptions, were built of wood as were the meeting-houses of other denominations. There are, however, certain common characteristics that divide the churches within this region into definite types depending more or less on the dates of their construction.

The first Anglican church in New England may be considered to have been the one built in 1607 at St. George's Fort, Maine. From the contemporary Spanish drawing in the Simancas Archives in Spain it would appear to have been built according to the old English crotch system in which the walls and roof were supported by pairs of forked posts set into the ground with the spaces between the framing probably filled with wattle and daub. The church apparently had a tower at the west end and was probably very much like the first two churches at Jamestown (1607, 1608) built in the same manner.[15] The first King's Chapel was the first of many small, simple, rectangular, frame structures of the late seventeenth and early eighteenth centuries which, except for their towers, have a rather close exterior resemblance to the contemporary, boxy, Puritan meeting-houses. The Price view of Boston of 1722 shows King's Chapel as having three windows, both on the north side and on the east end, with a low tower surmounted by a lofty finial bearing a crown and a weathercock. This can hardly be an accurate representation of the little building which had been enlarged in 1710 and which in its original form had dimensions 44 feet by 36 feet, with 5 windows on each side and 2 at each end, according to the contract for its construction. The document did specify 'on the west end of sd frame—one Belfry of ten feet square, twenty feet above ye roof.' It provided for windows with 'square glasse' and iron casements.[16] Since the belfry was to be on the west end of the frame it was not a tower in the usual sense of the word. As the principal door was in the middle of the south wall, it is assumed that the pulpit occupied the middle of the north wall opposite the door.

The first Trinity Church, Newport (1702), is believed to have had a similar plan, already shown to have been of frequent occurrence in Maryland and the Carolinas. St. Paul's Church, Wickford, Rhode Island (1707), although smaller, still retains a remarkably close resemblance to these other early structures (plates 96–7). St. Michael's, Marblehead (1714), also originally had its pulpit on the north wall with the chancel at the east end. Its belfry, which springs from the roof, is 50 feet high, but the 53-foot spire which had been planned never materialized. The present hipped roof of 1728 replaces an earlier medieval type of roof which had three gabled sections, side by side.

The first New England church of real architectural merit—Christ Church, Boston, built in 1723—is characteristic of the third type of structure, patterned in general after the churches developed by Sir Christopher Wren during the rebuilding of London after the great fire of 1666 (plates 100, 101). These are rectangular buildings with the chancel at the east end and a high pulpit with its sounding board placed directly in front of the altar at the end of the middle alley, or somewhat to the side of it. The fenestration occasionally consists of a single tier of tall arched windows where the gallery extends only across the rear of the nave; but most often there are two tiers of windows, thus allowing for galleries around three sides of the building to provide for a relatively large congregation, all within the compass of the preacher's voice. The roof pitch is relatively steep and the belfry and spire are carried on a distinct and separate tower built as an appendage of the main fabric at its west end. A splendid stone example is the present King's Chapel, Boston (plate 105), and fine wooden ones exist in the present Trinity Church, Newport (1725; plate 103), and Christ Church, Cambridge (1759; plate 109). The latter, like King's Chapel, was designed by Peter Harrison. The second St. Anne's Church, Gardiner, Maine (1793), closely resembled Christ Church.[17]

A later variation at the beginning of the nineteenth century forms the fourth type of New England church architecture in which the belfry and steeple rise from the main roof of the edifice in the manner of Gibbs, rather than that of Wren. This later group includes the majority of white churches whose slender spires rose from the elm-studded village greens of New England after 1800. The vestibule, with gallery stairs at each end, cuts across the front, leaving the audience room almost square. The galleries are on three sides with the end sometimes forming an ellipse. The pulpit, without a sounding board, began to be placed against the east wall with the altar table and font below it, forming a single liturgical center. Classic detail of cornices and moldings is lighter and more elaborate, windows have fewer lights in each sash, and the roof has a flatter pitch, with pedimented gable ends.

New England churches of the Georgian and early Federal periods, with only a few exceptions, are wooden structures that in themselves are remarkable examples of the adaptation of conventional architectural designs to available local materials. Timber was everywhere at hand. It was cheap and a medium in which local ship carpenters and joiners were highly skilled. Brick and lime were expensive, particularly in rural areas, and there was a scarcity of labor skilled in quarrying and laying stone. The frames were of heavy oak timbers, often a foot square, mortised and fastened together with wooden pins. Large crews of men were required to raise the frames with the aid of pike poles, screw jacks, and simple derricks with block and tackle and windlass. The raising of the tall spires was a particularly complicated feat of engineering and is described in detail by Norman M. Isham in his history of the great wooden Trinity Church at Newport.[18]

The clapboards were usually of pine, although those at St. Paul's, Woodbury, Connecticut (1785), are of split oak, beveled and lapped at the ends. The exterior doorways were naturally as important an architectural feature of these wooden buildings as they were of the brick churches of the South. The same classic pilasters and pediments frame the openings, but in New England they are of wood rather than the stone or rubbed brick used in the South. The paneled doors were made of white pine with iron hinges of H, L, or strap type terminating in spearheads. Finely wrought latch handles were used. The pure white that is now naturally identified with the typical New England church was not always characteristic. In the mid-eighteenth century Spanish brown, red, blue, and yellow, with trim in contrasting colors, were all used to paint churches. St. Matthew's in East Plymouth, Connecticut (1791), for example, was originally painted red.[19] Though the plaster walls and ceilings of the interiors were usually unpainted or white-washed, they were occasionally painted blue or green, and the box pews might be similarly painted. Christ Church, Bethany, Connecticut, in 1808 had white pews with red center panels inscribed with yellow Roman numerals, and the elaborate cornice below the ceiling was picked out in red, blue, green, gray, and cream. The city churches were, of course, relatively elaborate and might be extremely colorful. Poor country parish churches were sparsely furnished and sometimes could only boast of primitive decorations such as the chandelier of crimped tin that hangs in St. Matthew's at East Plymouth, Connecticut.

In the New England colonies a trend toward the Gothic Revival style in country churches seems to have preceded this tendency in the other states, probably a result of the fact that particularly in Connecticut the quarter century after the Revolution was a period of church building rather than one of decay. And much of the Gothic influence may be attributed to the use of simple Gothic forms in the Second Trinity Church in New York (plate 89).

While New England may take just pride in the antiquity and beauty of the imposing early churches that grace her cities, perhaps her greatest charm in an architectural sense lies in the small honest frame churches whose spires point heavenward above her quiet village greens. With these simple peculiarly American structures, we end our pilgrimage.

Episcopal Churches in New England which were Erected
before 1808 *and are still Standing:*

CONNECTICUT

1770	Old Trinity Church	Brooklyn	Windham County
1785	St. Paul's Church	Woodbury	Litchfield County
1786	Christ Church	Middle Haddam	New Haven County
1791	St. Matthew's Church	East Plymouth	Litchfield County
1797	Trinity Church	Seymour	New Haven County
1802	St. Peter's Church	Monroe	Fairfield County
1802	Trinity Church	Milton	Litchfield County
1803	Emanuel Church	Killingworth	Middlesex County
1806	St. Andrew's Church	Bloomfield	Hartford County

NEW HAMPSHIRE

1773	Union Church	West Claremont	Sullivan County
1797	Trinity Church	Holderness	Grafton County
1807	St. John's Church	Portsmouth	Rockingham County

RHODE ISLAND

1707	St. Paul's Church	Wickford	Washington County
1725	Trinity Church	Newport	Newport County

MASSACHUSETTS

1714	St. Michael's Church	Marblehead	Essex County
1723	Christ Church (Old North)	Boston	Suffolk County
1749	King's Chapel	Boston	Suffolk County
1759	Christ Church	Cambridge	Middlesex County

96. *St. Paul's Church, Wickford, Rhode Island,* 1707
(removed from Narragansett in 1800)

Five years after the first English Church was completed in Rhode Island, Trinity Church at Newport, this unimposing frame structure was built by the churchmen of Narragansett. In all probability, St. Paul's varies very little from the first Trinity Church at Newport, which may well have served as the model and which it is believed was patterned after the original King's Chapel in Boston. The latter was a simple wooden church built in 1687 with an interior plan thought to have been similar to St. Mildred's, Bread Street, which was finished in 1681 and was one of the simplest of Wren's London parish churches. According to the original contract, King's Chapel resembled St. Paul's, being five bays of windows in length and two in width. The first rector at Narragansett, the Reverend Christopher Bridge, was sent there by the Bishop of London after less than a year's service as assistant at King's Chapel.

97. *Interior—St. Paul's, Wickford*

In the three churches patterned after St. Mildred's, the altar was at the east end with the pulpit placed in the center of the north wall, and all eventually had galleries. Blocks of large pews occupied the middle of these churches. On the erection of the present Trinity Church at Newport, the altarpiece from the old church was supposed to be given to Narragansett, but whether or not it is the one seen above is pure conjecture.

98. *St. Michael's Church, Marblehead, Massachusetts,* 1714

The old seaport of Marblehead is the site of the second oldest Episcopal church standing in New England. The list of thirty-four original benefactors was headed by Colonel Francis Nicholson, whose deep interest in the expansion of the colonial Church once caused him to be spoken of by an S.P.G. missionary as 'fit to be a Bishop as to be a Governor.' Twenty-nine subscibers were sea captains. The church was aided by King's Chapel, Boston, although its early rectors received 'nothing from the people but the contributions collected after Divine Service on the Lord's Days at the Church.'

Today the interior of the hip-roofed little wooden structure has been much changed, but it contains many relics of its colorful history. The altarpiece was brought from England in 1714 when the church was built. The crucifix above it replaces the royal arms torn down by the mob when Marblehead had news of the Declaration of Independence. The organ originally came from the old St. Paul's Chapel in New York. The great brass 'candlestick' or chandelier was given in 1732 by John Elbridge, Collector of the Port of Bristol. For over two centuries, with the exception of the few years during the Revolution when the church was closed, the bell has rung out over the twisted streets of the historic town. It was recast by Paul Revere after having been rung for Independence until it cracked.

99. Interior—St. Michael's, Marblehead

100. *Christ Church ('Old North') Salem Street, Boston, Massachusetts, 1723*

It was in the belfry of the Old North Church that the two lights were hung on the night of 18 April 1775 when Paul Revere, whose statue now stands behind 'Old North,' and William Dawes rode through the Massachusetts countryside to warn the people that the king's troops were crossing the Charles River to move on supplies stored at Lexington.

Built in 1723 as a result of the missionary effort of the Society for the Propagation of the Gospel, 'Old North' was the first large church of the Wren type in New England. In spite of some faults of detail it was to all purposes a London parish church in brick.

Its two tiers of windows are in five bays, and its semicircular chancel is pierced by a great arched window. The brick building, laid in English bond, is 70 feet long, 51 feet wide, and the top of the spire is 175 feet from the ground. The tall spire served as a model for that of Trinity Church, Newport. The crypt beneath the church is believed to contain the remains of over one thousand persons in its thirty-seven vaults. Although this would not be unusual in an old London church, the extent to which Christ Church has been used for burials is unique among American churches. To enter the quiet building is to step into the atmosphere of a Wren church in London.

SAMUEL CHAMBERLAIN

101. *Interior—Christ Church, Boston*

The organ occupying the west gallery replaces the second instrument built by Thomas Johnston of Boston in 1759. The original case remains, with the addition of two end rows of pipes. The four carved wooden figures in front of the organ were presented in 1746 by Captain Gruchy of the privateer, *Queen of Hungary*, after he had captured them from a French vessel. They were en route to New France for use in a church in one of the settlements on the St. Lawrence. The brass 'branches' were given in 1724 by Captain William Maxwell.

In the eighteenth century the red loft, gilded organ pipes, and other fixtures lent colorful splendor to the interior. There are 106 pews in the church, numbered according to the plan of 1731. In 1802 it was voted that the middle pews should be lined with 'green stuff of any kind.' Directly behind the organ is the tower containing the first peal of eight bells brought to this country. The inscription on number eight states that 'Abel Rudhall of Gloucester cast us all. Anno 1744.' Number four proclaims 'God preserve the Church of England.'

ASA E. PHILLIPS, JR.

102. *Chancel—Christ Church, Boston*

The small altar table with massive turned legs is believed to have been part of the original furnishings. John Gibbs painted both the Ten Commandments and the king's arms in 1736. However, the paintings of the Last Supper, the Creed, and the Lord's Prayer were done by John Penniman in 1817. When they were placed in the chancel, the pulpit with its sounding board, which had been located at the end of the middle alley, was moved to the north so that the picture might be seen.

103. *Nave and Organ Gallery—Trinity Church, Newport, Rhode Island,* 1725

Trinity, Newport, is the only American church in which the pulpit remains in its original position directly in front of the chancel. This was once a common arrangement. Both Trinity and Christ Church, Boston, have somewhat similar vaulted ceilings, both were originally of almost identical dimensions (approximately 70 by 50 feet), and both contained five bays of arched windows in two tiers. Trinity Church was enlarged in 1762 by two additional bays. In its rear gallery opposite the sanctuary is the organ, topped, as in King's Chapel, by gilt miters. It was presented, according to the inscription in 1733, by 'Dr. George Berkeley late Lord Bishop of Cloyne' after his visit to the church in 1729.

104. *Pulpit and Chancel—Trinity Church, Newport*

The similarity between Trinity Church, Newport, and Christ Church, Boston, is so striking as to indicate that the former may be a wooden copy of the other—with minor intentional differences—or that both were built from the same set of drawings after one or more of Wren's London parish churches. Both churches were among the first fruits in New England of the work of the Society for the Propagation of the Gospel. The Trinity steeple is nearly an identical copy of that at Christ Church, and both interiors embody a curved chancel wall lighted by a great window over the altar.

WILLIAM KING COVELL

HASKELL

105. *King's Chapel, Boston, Massachusetts,* 1749

Although from 1686 until the War of Independence King's Chapel was a regular colonial parish of the Church of England, it took steps which separated it from the Anglican Communion in 1785 and later became the first Unitarian Church in America. It still uses its own revised version of the Book of Common Prayer and an order of service reflecting its traditions, however. In any event, a consideration of early Anglican churches in America would be incomplete if it did not give a prominent place to one of the most elegant examples of Georgian ecclesiastical architecture in America.

The cornerstone of the present stone structure was laid in 1749, but the chapel was not ready for use until 21 August 1754. On its completion, it had the most splendid church interior in New England. Fortunately, it was preserved with rare sympathy throughout the Victorian period that proved so dangerous to Georgian architecture.

Peter Harrison, architect of the building, planned to cap its squat western tower with a spire, but for some reason it was never undertaken. The portico of heavy wooden columns was not erected until 1785–7. Beside it is a monument to the Chevalier de Saint Sauveur, a young French officer who was killed in Boston in 1778 and is buried in the crypt of King's Chapel. The churchyard to the north of the building, which dates from 1630 and contains a gravestone alleged to be that of 'Mother Goose,' is the oldest burial place in Boston.

HASKELL

106. *The Pulpit—King's Chapel*

The 'three decker' pulpit, constructed in 1717, an inheritance from the earlier structure of 1688, is one of the oldest in the United States. Certainly from the number of great preachers of various denominations who have spoken from it on Sundays or at the famous noonday services of this city church, it is one of the most distinguished. Bishop Berkeley preached from it in 1731 and Charles Wesley in 1736, as did the Dean of St. Paul's Cathedral, London, in 1928—the first royal chaplain to have occupied the pulpit since 1775. The church is rich in memorials, including an unusual number of marble busts.

HASKELL

107. *View toward the Chancel—King's Chapel*

The carved and gilded altarpiece is believed to have been originally installed in the predecessor of the present structure. The four painted canvas panels embodied in it and carrying the Lord's Prayer, Decalogue, and Creed were 'drawn in England and brought over by Mr. Samuel Myles in July 1696' along with the altar table beneath them. The central window is modern.

The carved organ case of 1756 in the rear gallery is tastefully enriched with a crown and miters. According to tradition the instrument was selected by Handel. The interior of King's Chapel is beyond question of superb architectural quality. In the opinion of some critics it surpasses that of St. Paul's Chapel, New York, to stand as the finest church interior of the American colonies.

HASKELL

108. *The South Gallery—King's Chapel*

The superb twin Corinthian columns, dividing the church into five bays, rise from floor to ceiling and not only support the roof vaulting but the galleries abutting against them. Beneath the gallery in the second bay may be seen the smaller double columns at the corner of the restored governor's pew.

109. *Christ Church, Cambridge, Massachusetts, 1759*

Christ Church was organized in 1759 for Church of England families in Cambridge and students at Harvard College who had no church nearer than King's Chapel, Boston, then some ten miles away by road. The first S.P.G. missionary was the Reverend East Apthorp, a son of one of the greatest merchant princes of Boston, who had been educated in England and had taken holy orders there. Only twenty-six, he was of such brilliance and promise that he was suspected of having been privately selected to become the first bishop in the American colonies.

The church was opened for services 15 October 1761 and prospered until the Revolution. At the evacuation of Boston, practically all of the parishioners followed the British Army to Halifax and many went to England and never returned. After the battle of Lexington in 1775 the Church was used to shelter Revolutionary troops, although when Mrs. Washington joined the General in Cambridge in mid-December, she apparently took a great interest in the church. At her request a service was held in Christ Church 31 December 1775, the Washingtons and a number of others attending.

For many years after the Revolution the life of the parish was practically extinct, but by 1857 Christ Church had so revived that the church was cut in two and lengthened by two bays to accommodate the greatly enlarged congregations.

The gay red doors and gray exterior are the original colors of the church, which is largely built of oak. Timbers were cut on the upper Charles, floated down to Cambridge, and worked on the Common, where even the interior columns were turned. The building was designed by Peter Harrison of Yorkshire who had designed King's Chapel, the prototype of this simpler wooden edifice. In the Old Burying Ground next to the church, which belongs to the City of Cambridge, the first nine presidents of Harvard are buried as well as many soldiers of the Revolution and of all the colonial wars.

COURTESY LIBRARY OF CONGRESS

HASKELL

110. *Nave and Old Organ Loft—Christ Church, Cambridge*

The whole interior is characterized by an ordered simplicity of architectural detail. The box pews were replaced by slips in 1853. The original organ was built by Snetzler of London and procured for the church by Barlow Trecothick, Lord Mayor of London. During the Revolution some of the pipes were melted down to make bullets, and what remained was discarded for a new instrument in 1845.

111. *Old Trinity Church, Brooklyn, Connecticut,* 1770

The oldest Episcopal church in Connecticut was built by Godfrey Malbone, a graduate of King's College, Oxford, who came to Brooklyn from his native Newport in 1766 and bought some three thousand acres in the neighborhood. The plans of the structure—the only hip-roofed church still standing in Connecticut—were drawn by Malbone himself. The pulpit and reading desk originally stood in the middle alley in front of the altar. As a result, the pews, which are all of slip type with the exception of those on each side of the altar, become shorter as they approach the east end of the church.

Although the pulpit and reading desk have been moved and a reredos has been added, the interior appears much as it did originally. Its particular charm lies in its lack of pretense. The gallery and pews are unchanged. While the window frames and sash are original, the blinds are regrettable later additions. A Loyalist sympathizer, Malbone's quarrels with General Israel Putnam resulted in many tempestuous incidents in the town's history. Interestingly enough, his manor was later joined to the Putnam farm when a Malbone daughter married Daniel Putnam, the Revolutionary general's son.

112. *Union Church, Claremont, New Hampshire, 1773*

This oldest Episcopal church in New Hampshire was originally planned as a simple rectangle. The tower and belfry were not added until 1800. The plans are supposed to have been furnished by Governor John Wentworth who also promised to supply the nails and glass, but failed to keep his agreement. The main fabric remained unfinished for many years.

A large number of Tories lived in the Claremont area and, according to contemporary letters, churchmen were severely treated during the Revolution. The parish organization had been started in 1771 by the Reverend Samuel Peters of Hebron, Connecticut, although it was also served by the Reverend Ranna Cossit, a circuit rider furnished by the S.P.G. Cossit continued to minister to the parish during the war, but he was not allowed to go elsewhere in the colony and, it was claimed, received more insults than the Loyalists did. As a servant of the Society, it was believed by the Patriots that he propagated as much loyalty as he did religion.

Although the gallery at the rear has been removed, much of the interior is original, including the box pews topped by narrow railings set on spindles.

RICHARD M. COIT

113. *St. Peter's Church, Monroe, Connecticut, 1802*

If shingles had not replaced the original white clap-boards, St. Peter's would be generally characteristic of the wooden churches built throughout Connecti-cut during the eighteenth and early nineteenth cen-turies. It is reminiscent of the first Trinity Church, Hartford (1753-1817), except that it lacks its tall spire. The church faces north and has five bays of windows in two tiers—the windows of the second tier are arched—a fine paneled main doorway sur-mounted by a Palladian window, and a pleasing dentiled cornice. The open octagonal belfry was originally surrounded by a balustrade. Unfortunate-ly most of the original interior is gone, thanks to misguided Victorian enthusiasm for change.

114. *Trinity Church, Milton, Litchfield County, Connecticut, 1802*

This unusually interesting little building, which would benefit from repair, is an early example of the Gothic Revival churches that became so popular in New England during the first half of the nineteenth century. Although the roof is of relatively low pitch, the single tier of windows with Gothic heads and the steeple flanked by four pinnacles would appear to have been inspired by the Second Trinity Church, New York (1788–1839). Inside, the three galleries are supported by clustered colonettes of Gothic form, extending from floor to ceiling, and the sheathing of the gallery rails is ornamented by applied wooden strips in the form of alternate Gothic arches and quatrefoils. The ceiling, which is flat above the galleries, becomes a barrel vault over the center area of the nave. The fine mahogany and gilt organ case of 1823 was originally in St. Michael's, Litchfield.

115. *The Old Glebe House, Woodbury*

Here on 25 March 1783, at a secret meeting, ten of the fourteen Connecticut Church of England clergy elected the Reverend Jeremiah Leaming as their first choice to proceed to England for consecration as a bishop, with the Reverend Samuel Seabury as alternate. Because of ill health, Leaming declined and Seabury went in his place and was eventually consecrated by the Scottish bishops in 1784 as the first American bishop. The old house, an example of early eighteenth-century domestic architecture, is now maintained as a wayside shrine. During the Revolution, the Reverend John Rutgers Marshall, then the local rector, could not leave the house except on Sundays when, by law, there was immunity from arrest and he could hold public services. A sliding panel, discovered in the closet under the stair, has revealed his hiding place during the innumerable searches of the house made by the Patriots who came to arrest him on weekdays.

STEPHEN P. DORSEY

STEPHEN P. DORSEY

116. *West Doorway—Trinity, Milton*

The doorway is of special interest in its combination of classic and Gothic form and detail. The Gothic arched opening is framed by pilasters which are decorated with applied Gothic tracery, but which have classic capitals and bases and support a classic architrave and cornice.

117. *Interior, St. John's, Portsmouth*

Although the frescoed walls, Victorian slip pews, and altered floor plan are distracting elements, the interior of this church still shows the simplicity of line and classic motifs that are characteristic of most New England churches built during the early Federal Period. The inscribed panels of the handsome altar piece are hidden by the white draperies used on Easter morning, but the quality and refinement of its carved and fluted frame are evident.

DOUGLAS ARMSDEN

118. *St. John's Church, Portsmouth, New Hampshire, 1807*

Portsmouth, the former capital of New Hampshire, is known for the fine Georgian and Federal houses built by its early merchants. It possesses a similar treasure in St. John's Church, built in 1807 on the site of the former Queen's Chapel, which had been erected in 1732 under the auspices of the S.P.G. The severity of this brick structure of five bays is relieved by the refinement of its octagonal wooden cupola. When the old wooden chapel of the royal governors of New Hampshire burned in 1806, its bell, which had been captured from the French at Louisburg by Colonel Pepperell of Kittery Point, was cracked. It was sent to Boston and was recast by Paul Revere. Recast again in 1896, it still rings out above Portsmouth as it once did from a French church on the stormy Cape Breton coast.

The church owns a chancel chair and Bible as well as Prayer Books and altar plate presented by Queen Caroline, Consort of George II. The great marble font was taken from the French at the capture of Senegal in 1758 by Captain John Mason and was presented to the church by his daughters in 1761. The rectory may be seen next to the church.

DOUGLAS ARMSDEN

NOTES

I. HISTORICAL BACKGROUND

1. Perry, W. S., *The History of the American Episcopal Church*, Boston, 1885, I, pp. 45, 46.
2. Ibid. p. 2.
3. Hening, W. W., *The Statutes at Large; Being a Collection of All the Laws of Virginia, from the First Session of the Legislature, in the year 1619*, New York, 1823, I, pp. 68, 69.
4. Suter, J. W. and Cleaveland, G. J., *The American Book of Common Prayer*, New York, 1949, p. 48.
5. Brydon, G. M., *Virginia's Mother Church*, Richmond, 1947, p. 25.
6. Manross, W. W., *History of the American Episcopal Church*, New York, 1935, p. 15.
7. Pennington, E. L., *Apostle of New Jersey, John Talbot*, Philadelphia, 1938, pp. 74, 75, 78.
8. Wakeman, N. O., *The History of the Church of England*, London, 1920, p. 410.
9. Pascoe, C. F., *Two Hundred Years of the Society for the Propagation of the Gospel, 1701–1900*, London, 1901, II, pp. 932–5. The charter, which is in the Society's archives, is here printed in full.
10. Chorley, E. C., 'The Seal of the Society for the Propagation of the Gospel,' *Historical Magazine of the Protestant Episcopal Church*, September 1943, p. 253.
11. Klingberg, F. J., 'Contributions of the Society for the Propagation of the Gospel to the American Way of Life,' *Historical Magazine of the Protestant Episcopal Church*, September 1943, pp. 220–21.
12. Ibid. p. 220.
13. Wakeman, op. cit. p. 413.
14. Manross, op. cit. p. 173.
15. Ibid. p. 172.
16. Suter and Cleaveland, op. cit. p. 54.

II. CHURCH INTERIORS AND THEIR ORNAMENTS

1. Addleshaw, G. W. O. and Etchells, F., *The Architectural Setting of Anglican Worship*, London, 1948, p. 15.
2. Ibid. pp. 16–18.
3. Ibid. pp. 24, 28–9.
4. Frere, W. H., *Visitation Articles and Injunctions of the Period of the Reformation*, London, 1910, III, pp. 62, 109.
5. Ibid. III, p. 109.
6. Addleshaw and Etchells, op. cit. pp. 39–41.
7. Mason, G. C., *Colonial Churches of Tidewater, Virginia*, Richmond, 1945, pp. 169, 287–8.
8. Ibid. p. 248.
9. Strachey, W., *Purchas his Pilgrimes*, Glasgow, 1905, XIX, p. 56.
10. Addleshaw and Etchells, op. cit. p. 66.
11. Mason, op. cit. p. 46.
12. Updike, W., *History of the Episcopal Church in Narragansett, Rhode Island*, Boston, 1907, II, p. 473.
13. Addleshaw and Etchells, op. cit. pp. 82–4.
14. Ibid. p. 90.
15. Mason, op. cit. p. 239.
16. Ibid. p. 179.
17. Maryland Historical Records Survey Project, *Inventory of the Church Archives of Maryland*, Baltimore, 1940, p. 153.

18. Dix, M., *The Parish of Trinity Church in the City of New York*, New York, 1898, I, p. 217.
19. Dearmer, P., *The Art of Public Worship*, London, 1919, p. 119.
20. Pepys, S., *Diary of Samuel Pepys*, London, 1930, pp. 185-6.
21. Legg, J. W., *English Church Life from the Restoration to the Tractarian Movement*, London, 1941, pp. 185-6.
22. Babcock, M. K. D., 'The Organs and Organ Builders of Christ Church, Boston, 1736-1945,' *The Historical Magazine of the Protestant Episcopal Church*, September 1945, pp. 246-7.
23. Dix, op. cit. I, pp. 305, 316, 338, 339.
24. Babcock, op. cit. p. 246.
25. Addleshaw and Etchells, op. cit. p. 101.
26. Godolphin, J., *Repertorium Canonicum*, 1678, p. 9.
27. Dix, op. cit. I, p. 219.
28. Kelly, J. F., *Early Connecticut Meeting Houses*, New York, 1948, p. xlviii.
29. Forman, H. G., *Jamestown and St. Mary's*, Baltimore, 1938, p. 250.
30. Addleshaw and Etchells, op. cit. pp. 146-50.
31. Ibid. p. 121.
32. Addleshaw and Etchells, op. cit. p. 155.
33. Ibid. p. 156.
34. Ibid. p. 158.
35. Writers' Program, Works Progress Administration, Maryland, *Maryland, A Guide to the Old Line State*, New York, 1940, p. 474.
36. Meade, W., *Old Churches, Ministers and Families of Virginia*, Philadelphia, 1857, I, p. 323.
37. Mason, op. cit. p. 38.
38. Meade, op. cit. p. 323.
39. *Handbook of Pohick Church*, Truro Parish, Fairfax County, Virginia, p. 5.
40. Foote, H. W., *Annals of King's Chapel*, Boston, 1882, I, p. 212.
41. Addleshaw and Etchells, op. cit. p. 168.
42. Mason, op. cit. p. 17.
43. See Royal Commission on Historical Monuments, *An Inventory of the Historical Monuments in London*, London, 1925, II, Plates 27, 206, for illustrations.
44. Addleshaw and Etchells, op. cit. p. 170.
45. See Royal Commission on Historical Monuments, *An Inventory of the Historical Monuments in the City of Oxford*, London, 1939, Plate 105.
46. Greenwood, F. P., *The History of King's Chapel*, Boston, 1833, p. 53.
47. Meade, op. cit. I, p. 45.
48. Dearmer, P., *The Ornaments of the Ministers*, New York, 1922, p. 90.
49. Cox, J. D., and Harvey, A., *English Church Furniture*, New York, 1907, p. 343.
50. Acrelius, I., *A History of New Sweden, or The Settlements on the Delaware*, translated from the Swedish by W. M. Reynolds, Philadelphia, 1894, p. 359.
51. Meade, op. cit. I, p. 82.
52. Writers' Program, Works Progress Administration, *Maryland*, op. cit. p. 466.
Seymour, G. D., *The Reverend Jeremiah Leaming of Connecticut*, New Haven, 1928, p. 30.
53. Meade, op. cit. I, p. 35.

III. CHURCHES OF THE COLONIAL ESTABLISHMENT IN VIRGINIA AND MARYLAND

1. Manross, W. W., *A History of the American Episcopal Church*, New York, 1935, p. 12.
2. Brydon, G. M., *Virginia's Mother Church*, Richmond, 1947, p. 135.
3. Ibid. p. 144.
4. Historical Records Survey, *Inventory of the Church Archives of Maryland*, Baltimore, 1940, pp. 7, 12, 17.
5. Manross, op. cit. pp. 70, 75.
6. Jones, H. *Of the State of the Church and Clergy of Virginia*, London, 1724, p. 97.
7. Manross, op. cit. p. 77.
8. Brydon, op. cit. p. 249.
9. Manross, op. cit. p. 77. *Inventory of the Church Archives of Maryland*, op. cit. p. 22.
10. Manross, op. cit. p. 181.
11. Meade, W., *Old Churches, Ministers and Families of Virginia*, Philadelphia, 1857, I, pp. 17, 56.

12. *St. Peter's Parish, New Kent County, Virginia, Vestry Book,* 1685–1758, photostat copy in Archives Department, Virginia State Library, entry for 18 November 1719.
13. Waterman, T. T., 'The Bruton Church of 1683 and Two Contemporaries,' *Journal of the American Society of Architectural Historians,* July–October 1944, pp. 43–6.

14. Forman, op. cit. p. 250.
15. Mason, op. cit. p. 299.
16. Ibid. pp. 47, 48.
17. Ibid. pp. 12, 13.
18. Ibid. pp. 172, 173, 111, 114, 115.
19. *Inventory of the Church Archives of Maryland,* op. cit. pp. 153, 154.

IV. CHURCHES OF THE COLONIAL ESTABLISHMENT IN THE CAROLINAS

1. Manross, W. W., *History of the American Episcopal Church,* New York, 1935, pp. 81, 82. Stoney, S. G., *Plantations of the Carolina Low Country,* Charleston, 1938, p. 20.
2. *Society for the Propagation of the Gospel in Foreign Parts,* Series A, XXIII, Transcript in the Library of Congress, Manuscript Division.
3. Manross, op. cit. p. 85.
4. Graham, J. W., *History of St. Paul's Episcopal Church,* Edenton, 1936, p. 5.
5. Manross, op. cit. p. 87.
6. Stoney, op. cit. p. 26.
7. Manross, op. cit. pp. 105, 151.
8. Ibid. pp. 89, 90.

9. Society for the Propagation of the Gospel in Foreign Parts, *Letters and Reports of the Missionaries and Other Correspondents in the American Colonies,* Series B, XX, p. 132.
10. Johnston, F. B. and Waterman, T. T., *The Early Architecture of North Carolina,* Chapel Hill, 1931, p. 245.
11. Ibid. p. 245.
12. National Park Service, *Historical American Buildings Survey,* Washington, 1941, North Carolina (10).
13. Howe, G. G., *History of St. Philip's Church,* Charleston, p. 3.

V. EARLY EPISCOPAL CHURCHES OF THE MIDDLE STATES

1. Fleming, F. S., Historical introduction in *250th Anniversary of the Parish of Trinity Church in the City of New York* (Catalogue of the Commemorative Exhibition of Historical Treasures at the New-York Historical Society), New York, 1947, pp. 8, 9.
2. Manross, W. W., *A History of the American Episcopal Church,* New York, 1935, p. 113.
3. Ibid. p. 122.
4. Eberlein, H. D. and Hubbard, C. V. D., *Historic Houses of the Hudson Valley,* New York, 1942, p. 68.
5. Dix, M., *The Parish of Trinity Church in the City of New York,* New York, 1898, I, pp. 270–76.
6. Ibid. I, p. 275.

7. Rightmyer, N. W., *The Anglican Church in Delaware,* Philadelphia, 1947, pp. 5, 6.
8. Manross, op. cit. p. 132.
9. Klingberg, F. J., 'Religious Society on the Delaware in 1708 as seen by Thomas Jenkins, *Historical Magazine of the Protestant Episcopal Church,* March 1945, pp. 66–73.
10. Historical Records Survey, *Inventory of the Church Archives of New Jersey, Protestant Episcopal Diocese of Newark,* Newark, 1939, p. 16.
11. Manross, op. cit. pp. 127, 129, 135.
12. Historical Records Survey, New Jersey, op. cit. p. 16.
13. Manross, op. cit. pp. 180, 181.
14. Rightmyer, op. cit. p. 145.
15. Ibid. p. 145.

VI. EARLY EPISCOPAL CHURCHES IN NEW ENGLAND

1. Manross, W. W., *A History of the American Episcopal Church*, New York, 1935, p. 28.
2. *One Hundredth Anniversary of the Diocese of Maine*, Gardiner, 1920, pp. 26, 27.
3. Manross, op. cit. p. 28.
4. Foote, H. W., *Annals of King's Chapel, Boston, 1882–1940*, III, p. 15.
5. Manross, op. cit. p. 31.
6. Ibid. p. 97.
7. Babcock, M. K. D., 'Difficulties and Dangers of Pre-Revolutionary Ordinations,' *Historical Magazine of the Protestant Episcopal Church*, September 1943, pp. 226–40.
8. Manross, op. cit. p. 104.
9. Kelly, J. F., *Early Connecticut Meeting Houses*, New York, 1948, xxxiii.
10. Manross, op. cit. pp. 98, 99, 105, 106.
11. Ibid. pp. 107, 109.
    One Hundredth Anniversary of the Diocese of Maine, op. cit. pp. 27–9.
12. Mapoteng, C., 'The Rev. William Clark (1740–1815), S.P.G. Missionary in Massachusetts,' *Historical Magazine of the Protestant Episcopal Church*, June 1947, p. 208.
13. Manross, op. cit. p. 175.
14. Mapoteng, op. cit. pp. 212–14.
    Seymour, G. D., *The Reverend Jeremiah Leaming*, Woodbury, Conn., 1928, pp. 11–13.
15. Mason, G. C., *Colonial Churches of Tidewater Virginia*, Richmond, 1945, p. 3 (see also the preceding chapter on Churches of the Colonial Establishment in Virginia and Maryland).
16. Isham, N. M., *Trinity Church in Newport, Rhode Island*, Boston, 1936, p. 8.
17. *One Hundredth Anniversary of the Diocese of Maine*, op. cit. p. 55.
18. Isham, op. cit. pp. 97–103.
19. Kelly, op. cit. p. xlvii.

BIBLIOGRAPHY

(Articles from the proceedings of learned societies and mono-
graphs on particular churches of pertinent interest are included.)

I. THE GENERAL HISTORICAL AND ARCHITECTURAL BACKGROUND

Addleshaw, G.W.O. and Etchells, F., *The Architec-tural Setting of Anglican Worship*, London, 1948.

Anderson, J.S.M., *The History of the Church of Eng-land*, London, 1845–56.

Andrews, C.M. and Davenport, F.G., *Manuscript Materials in the British Museum for the History of the United States to 1783*, Washington, 1908.

Babcock, M.K.D., 'Difficulties and Dangers of Pre-Revolutionary Ordinations,' *Historical Mag-azine of the Protestant Episcopal Church*, Sep-tember 1943.

Batsford, H. and Fry, C., *The Cathedrals of England*, New York, 1940.

Batsford, H. and Fry, C., *The Greater English Church of the Middle Ages*, New York, 1940.

Bennett, G.F., *Early Architecture of Delaware*, Wil-mington, 1932.

Birch, G.H., *London Churches of the XVIIth and XVIIIth Centuries*, London, 1896.

The Booke of the Common Prayer and Administracion of the Sacramentes, London, 1549 (a reprint *verbatim et literatim* by Griffith Farran Browne and Co., Ltd., London).

The Boke of Common Prayer and Administracion of the Sacramentes, London, 1552 (a reprint *verbatim et literatim* by Griffith Farran Okeden and Welsh, London).

Bumpus, T.F., *Ancient London Churches*, London, 1923.

Cobb, Gerald, *The Old Churches of London*, London, 1948.

Combe, W., *A History of the University of Cam-bridge*, London, 1815.

Coulton, G.C., *Medieval Panorama*, Cambridge, 1938.

Cox, J.C. and Harvey, A., *English Church Furniture*, New York, 1907.

Dearmer, P., *The Art of Public Worship*, London, 1919.

Dearmer, P., *The Ornaments of the Ministers*, London and Oxford, 1920.

Dowley, P.M., *Chapters in Church History*, New York, 1950.

Dugdale, W., *History of St. Paul's Cathedral in Lon-don with a Continuation by Henry Ellis*, Lon-don, 1818.

Ellwood, G.M., and Day, E.H., *Some London Churches*, London, 1911.

Embury, A., *Early American Churches*, Garden City, 1914.

Frere, W.H., *Visitation Articles and Injunctions of the Period of the Reformation*, London, 1910.

Godolphin, J., *Repertorium Canonicum*, London, 1678.

Hening, W.W., *The Statutes at Large; Being a col-lection of all the Laws of Virginia, from the First Session of the Legislature in the Year 1619*, 13 vols., New York, 1823.

Hollis, G., *How the Church Was Reformed in England*, Milwaukee, 1920.

Jackson, W., *The Ornaments of Churches Considered*, Oxford, 1761.

Klingberg, F.K., 'Contributions of the S.P.G. to the American Way of Life,' *Historical Magazine of the Protestant Episcopal Church*, September 1943.

Lancaster, F., *A Geneological History of the Kings of England*, London, 1683.

Legg, J.W., *English Church Life from the Restoration to the Tractarian Movement*, London, 1914.

MacColl, M., *The Royal Commission and the Ornaments Rubric*, London, 1906.

Manross, W.W., *The Episcopal Church in the United States, 1800–1840*, New York, 1938.

Manross, W.W., *A History of the American Episcopal Church*, New York, 1935.

Muller, J.A., 'George Keith (1638–1716) First S.P.G. Missionary to America,' *Historical Magazine of the Protestant Episcopal Church*, June 1944.

National Park Service, *Historic American Buildings Survey*, Washington, 1944.

Pascoe, C.F., *Two Hundred Years of the S.P.G., 1701–1900*, London, 1901.

Pepys, S., *Diary of Samuel Pepys*, London, 1930.

Perry, W.S., *The History of the American Episcopal Church*, Boston, 1885.

Pyne, W.H., *The History of the Royal Residences*, London, 1819.

Royal Commission on Historical Monuments, *An Inventory of the Historical Monuments in London*, London, 1925.

Royal Commission on Historical Monuments, *An Inventory of the Historical Monuments in the City of Oxford*, London, 1939.

Royal Institute of British Architects, London, *Sir Christopher Wren, A.D. 1632–1723*, London, 1923.

Society for the Propagation of the Gospel in Foreign Parts, *Letters and Reports of the Missionaries and Other Correspondents in the American Colonies*, Series A, vols. I–XXVI. *Contemporary copies of letters received 1702–1736, chiefly from the American colonies . . .*, Transcripts, Series B, vols I–XXV. *Original letters received from the American colonies . . . 1702–1799*, Transcripts (Library of Congress Manuscript Division).

Sparrow, A., *Collections of Articles, Injunctions, Canons, Orders, Ordinances and Constitutions Ecclesiastical of the Church of England*, London, 1675.

Strachey, W., *Purchas his Pilgrimes*, Glasgow, 1905.

Suter, J.W. and Cleaveland, G.J., *The American Book of Common Prayer*, New York, 1949.

Thompson, A.H., *The Historical Growth of the English Parish Church*, London, 1911.

Tiffany, C. C., *History of the Protestant Episcopal Church in the United States of America*, New York, 1895.

Upjohn, H.B., *Churches in Eight American Colonies Differing in Elements of Design*, New York, 1925.

Wakeman, H.O., *An Introduction to the History of the Church of England, from the Earliest Times to the Present Day*, London, 1920.

Wallace, P.B., *Colonial Churches and Meeting Houses, Pennsylvania, New Jersey and Delaware. . . .* Measured Drawings by William Allen Dunn, New York, 1931.

Wilson, T., *The Ornaments of Churches Considered*, Oxford, 1761.

Wren, Sir C., *The Parochial Churches of Sir Christopher Wren, 1666–1718*, Oxford, 1932–3, 2 vols.

Wren, Sir C., *The Works of Sir Christopher Wren. The Dimensions, Plans, Elevations, and Sections of the Parochial Churches of Sir Christopher Wren, Erected in the Cities of London & Westminster. By John Clayton, architect*, London, 1848 and 1849.

II. THE REGIONS AND INDIVIDUAL CHURCHES

Allen, E., *The Garrison Church*, New York, 1898.

Babcock, M.K.D., 'The Organs and Organ Builders of Christ Church, Boston, 1736–1945,' *The Historical Magazine of the Protestant Episcopal Church*, September 1945.

Beardsley, W.A., 'The Episcopate of Bishop Seabury,' *Historical Magazine of the Protestant Episcopal Church*, September 1934.

Brock, H.I., *Colonial Churches in Virginia*, Richmond, 1930.

Bruton Parish Church, A Brief History, Williamsburg, Virginia.

Brydon, G.M., *The Clergy of the Established Church in Virginia and the Revolution*, Richmond, 1933 (Virginia Historical Magazine).

—*Virginia's Mother Church and the Political Conditions Under Which it Grew*, Richmond, 1947.

Burgess, J.M., *Chronicles of St. Mark's Parish, Santee Circuit, and Williamsburg Township, South Carolina, 1731–1885*, Columbia, S.C., 1888.

Chambers, B.D., *Old Chapel and the Parish in Clarke County, Virginia*, Washington, 1932.

Chorley, E.C., 'The Beginnings of the Church in the Province of New York,' *The Historical Magazine of the Protestant Episcopal Church*, March 1944.

Christ Church, Salem Street, Boston, 1723, A Guide, Boston, 1944.

Dalcho, Frederick, *An Historical Account of the Protestant Episcopal Church in South Carolina*, Charleston, 1820.

Davis, F.W., 'Old St. John's Parish,' reprinted from *New England Magazine*, November 1894.

De Mille, G.E., *A History of the Diocese of Albany, 1704–1923*, Philadelphia, 1946.

Dix, M., *The Parish of Trinity Church in the City of New York*, New York, 1898.

Eberlein, H.D. and Hubbard, C.V., *The Church of St. Peter in the Great Valley, 1700–1940*, Richmond, 1944.

—*Historic Houses of the Hudson Valley*, New York, 1942.

Foote, H.W., *Annals of King's Chapel*, Boston, 1882–1940, 3 vols.

Forman, H.C., *Jamestown and St. Mary's*, Baltimore, 1938.

Goodwin, M.F., 'Alexander Moray—First Bishop Designate of Virginia, 1672–3,' *The Historical Magazine of the Protestant Episcopal Church*, March 1943.

Graham, J.W., *History of St. Paul's Episcopal Church*, Edenton, 1936.

Greenwood, F.P., *The History of King's Chapel*, Boston, 1833.

Handbook of Pohick Church, Truro Parish, Fairfax County, Virginia.

Hanson, G.A., *Old Kent: the Eastern Shore of Maryland . . . and the Parishes of St. Paul's, Shrewsbury and I. U.*, Baltimore, 1876.

Haywood, M.D., *Lives of the Bishops of North Carolina*, Raleigh, 1910.

Historical Records Survey, Connecticut, *Inventory of the Church Archives of Connecticut, Protestant Episcopal*, New Haven, 1940.

Historical Records Survey, District of Columbia, *Inventory of Church Archives in the District of Columbia . . . The Protestant Episcopal Church Diocese of Washington*, vol. 1, District of Columbia, Montgomery, Prince Georges, Charles, St. Mary's Counties, Maryland, Washington, 1940.

Historical Records Survey, Maryland, *Inventory of the Church Archives of Maryland, Protestant Episcopal, Diocese of Maryland*, Baltimore, 1940.

Historical Records Survey, Massachusetts, *A Description of the Manuscript Collections in the Massachusetts Diocesan Library*, Boston, 1939.

Historical Records Survey, New Jersey, *Inventory of the Church Archives of New Jersey Protestant Episcopal Diocese of Newark*, Newark, 1939.

Historical Records Survey, New York City, *Inventory of the Church Archives of New York City. Protestant Episcopal Church, Diocese of Long Island*, New York, 1940.

Historical Records Survey, New York City, *Inventory of the Church Archives of New York City. Protestant Episcopal Church of the United States of America Diocese of New York, Manhattan, Bronx, Richmond*, New York, 1940.

Historical Records Survey, New York State, *Inventory of the Church Archives of New York State Exclusive of New York City. Protestant Episcopal Church Diocese of Rochester*, Albany, 1941.

Historical Records Survey, New York (State), *Inventory of the Church Archives of New York State, Exclusive of New York City, Protestant Episcopal Church Diocese of Western New York*, Albany, 1939.

Historical Records Survey, New Hampshire, *Inventory of the Church Archives of New Hampshire, Protestant Episcopal Diocese of New Hampshire*, Manchester, 1942.

Historical Records Survey, Vermont, *Inventory of the Church Archives of Vermont*, vol. 1, Diocese of Vermont, Protestant Episcopal, Montpelier, 1940.

Historical Records Survey, West Virginia, *Inventory of the Church Archives of West Virginia . . . The Protestant Episcopal Church*, Wheeling, 1939.

Historical Society of Delaware, *The Records of Holy Trinity (Old Swedes) Church, Wilmington, Delaware from 1697 to 1773*, Wilmington, 1893.

Howe, G.C., *History of St. Philip's Church*, Charleston.

In Commemoration of the 250th Anniversary Year, Christ Church in Philadelphia, Philadelphia, 1945.

Isham, N.M., *Trinity Church in Newport, Rhode Island*, Boston, 1936.

Johnston, F.B., *The Early Architecture of North Carolina, a Pictorial Survey . . . with an architectural history by T. T. Waterman*, Chapel Hill, 1947.

Kelly, J.F., *Early Connecticut Meeting Houses*, New York, 1948.

Klingberg, F.J., 'Religious Society on the Delaware in 1708 as seen by Thomas Jenkins,' *Historical Magazine of the Protestant Episcopal Church*, March 1945, pp. 66–73.

Linsley, G.J., *The Old Glebe House of Woodbury Connecticut, An Historical Address*, Hartford, 1925.

Lydekker, J.W., 'Thomas Bray,' *The Historical Magazine of the Protestant Episcopal Church*, September 1943.

McCrady, E., *An Historic Church. The Westminster Abbey of South Carolina. A sketch of St. Philip's Church, Charleston, S.C., 1665 to the present time . . .*, Charleston, 1897.

McKim, R.H., *Washington's Church*, Alexandria, 1886.

Marlowe, G.F., *Churches of Old New England*, New York, 1947.

Mason, G.C., *Colonial Churches of Tidewater Virginia*, Richmond, 1945.

Mathews, J.T., *The Romance of Old Christ Church, Alexandria, Virginia*, Washington, 1926.

Meade, W., *Old Churches, Ministers and Families of Virginia*, Philadelphia, 1861, 2 vols.

Merritt, E., *Old Wye Church, Talbot County, Maryland*, Baltimore, 1949.

New-York Historical Society, *250th Anniversary of the Parish of Trinity Church in the City of New York* (Catalogue of the Commemorative Exhibition of Historical Treasures), New York, 1947.

One Hundredth Anniversary of the Diocese of Maine, Gardiner, 1920.

Pennington, E.L., *Apostle of New Jersey, John Talbot*, Philadelphia, 1938.

Perry, W.S., *Papers Relating to the History of the Church in Virginia, A.D. 1650–1776*, Hartford, 1870.

Protestant Episcopal Church in the U.S.A. *New York Diocese Committee on Historical Publications Centennial History of the Protestant Episcopal Church in the Diocese of New York, 1785–1885*, New York, 1886.

Ridgeley, H.W., *The Old Brick Churches of Maryland*, New York, 1894.

Rightmyer, N.W., *The Anglican Church in Delaware*, Philadelphia, 1947.

Rines, E.F., *Old Historic Churches of America*, New York, 1936.

Rodney, R.S., 'Immanuel Church—Newcastle, Delaware,' *Historical Magazine of the Protestant Episcopal Church*, December 1943.

Seymour, G.D., *The Reverend Jeremiah Leaming of Connecticut*, New Haven, 1928.

Shinn, G.W., *King's Handbook of Notable Episcopal Churches in the United States*, Boston, 1889.

Skivern, P.G., *The First Parishes of the Province of Maryland*, Baltimore, 1923.

Slaughter, P., *The History of Truro Parish in Virginia*, Philadelphia, 1908.

Southern Churchman, *Colonial Churches; a Series of Sketches of Churches in the Original Colony of Virginia*, Richmond, 1907.

Stevens, W.B., *The Building of a Diocese*, Philadelphia, 1884.

Stoney, S.G., *Plantations of the Carolina Low Country*, Charleston, 1938.

Two Hundred Twenty-Fifth Anniversary, St. Paul's Episcopal Church, Rock Creek Parish, Washington, D.C., 1944.

Updike, W., *History of the Episcopal Church in Narragansett, Rhode Island*, Boston, 1907, 3 vols.

Wallington, N.U., *Historic Churches of America*, New York, 1907.

Waterman, T.T., 'The Bruton Church of 1683 and Two Contemporaries,' *Journal of the American Society of Architectural Historians*, July-October 1944.

Waterman, T.T., *The Mansions of Virginia*, 1706–1776, Chapel Hill, 1946.

Wilstach, P., *Potomac Landings*, Garden City, 1921.

Wilstach, P., *Tidewater Maryland*, Indianapolis, 1931.

Wilstach, P., *Tidewater Virginia*, Indianapolis, 1929.

Wootten, Mrs. B.M., *Charleston; Azaleas and Old Bricks . . .*, text by S. G. Stoney, Boston, 1937.

Wootten, Mrs. B.M., *New Castle Delaware 1651–1939 . . .*, text by Anthony Higgins, Boston, 1939.

Writers' Program, Connecticut, *Connecticut, A Guide to Its Roads, Lore and People*, Boston, 1938.

Writers' Program, Delaware, *Delaware, A Guide to the First State*, New York, 1938.

Writers' Program, Georgia, *Georgia, A Guide to its Towns and Countryside*, Athens, 1940.

Writers' Program, Maine, *Maine, A Guide 'Down East,'* Boston, 1937.

Writers' Program, Maryland, *Maryland, A Guide to the Old Line State*, New York, 1940.

Writers' Program, Massachusetts, *Massachusetts, A Guide to its Places and People*, Boston, 1937.

Writers' Program, New Hampshire, *New Hampshire, A Guide to the Granite State*, Boston, 1938.

Writers' Program, New Jersey, *New Jersey, A Guide to its Present and Past*, New York, 1939.

Writers' Program, New York, *New York, A Guide to the Empire State*, Oxford, 1940.

Writers' Program, New York (City), *New York City Guide; A Comprehensive Guide to the Five Boroughs of the Metropolis*, New York, 1939.

Writers' Program, North Carolina, *North Carolina, A Guide to the Old North State*, Chapel Hill, 1939.

Writers' Program, Pennsylvania, *Pennsylvania, A Guide to the Keystone State*, New York, 1940.

Writers' Program, Rhode Island, *Rhode Island, A Guide to the Smallest State*, Boston, 1937.

Writers' Program, South Carolina, *South Carolina, A Guide to the Palmetto State*, New York, 1941.

Writers' Program, Vermont, *Vermont, A Guide to the Green Mountain State*, Boston, 1937.

Writers' Program, Virginia, *Virginia, A Guide to the Old Dominion*, New York, 1940.

Writers' Program, West Virginia, *West Virginia, A Guide to the Mountain State*, New York, 1941.

INDEX

organs, 24, 64, 83, 105, 133, 138, 145, 168, 172, 174, 182, 188
orientation of churches, 45, 116
Oxford Movement, 17
Oxford University, 3, 6, 22, 30, 44, 63, 183

P

painters, 29, 82, 173
Parker, Samuel (Bishop), 162
Petsworth Church, Gloucester County, Va., 29, 30
pews, 22-4, 35, 63, 73, 82, 109, 167, 172, 174, 179, 183, 184
plans, cruciform, 44, 46, 47, 56, 60, 76, 78, 91, 94, 117, 123
    rectangular, 45, 59, 91, 116, 118, 162, 184
    T and L, 45, 56
Pohick Church, Fairfax County, Va., 47, 51, 78, 83, 84, 85
Pompion Hill Chapel, Berkeley County, S.C., 21, 22, 92, 93, 106-9
porches, 47, 57, 70, 80, 117, 163
porticoes, 91, 92, 102, 142, 176
Prayer, Lord's, 29, 30, 81, 173, 178; *see also* tablets of the Law
prayers, altar, 20
Presbyterians, 41, 87, 111, 112
Prince George's Chapel, Dagsboro, Del., 116, 119
Prince William's Church, Sheldon, S.C., 91
Protestant Episcopal Church in the United States, 9, 10, 11
Provoost, Samuel (Bishop), 10, 13, 42, 115, 149
psalms, 24
pulpits, 19-21, 55, 68, 74, 78, 105, 108, 109, 132, 138, 144, 153, 155, 173, 174, 177
Pungoteague Church, Accomac County, Va., 46, 50
Puritans, 2-4, 8, 15, 24, 32, 39, 157, 160

Q

Quakers, 5, 41, 87, 160, 161

R

rails, altar, 28, 36, 83
Ratcliffe, Rev. Robert, 159
reading desks, 19-21, 68, 138, 153, 183
Reformation, 2, 32
requests for American Episcopate, 8, 40, 41, 114, 123, 162
reredoses, *see* altarpieces

Restoration, 4-6, 24, 28, 40
Revere, Paul, 168, 170
Roman Catholic Chapel, St. Mary's, Md., 44
Roman Catholics, 2, 4, 5, 40, 41, 44, 87
rood lofts, 16
roofs, flared, 66, 72, 80
    gable, 57, 122, 163, 186
    hip, 70, 80, 85, 90, 163, 168, 183
    jerkin-head, 91, 92
royal arms, 24, 25, 68, 89, 96, 168, 173
Rudman, Rev. Andreas, 115, 123

S

St. Andrew's Church, Bloomfield, Conn., 165
    Leonardtown, Md., 47, 48, 52, 82, 91
    Princess Anne, Md., 52
    St. Andrew's Parish, S.C., 91, 93, 94
    Surry County, Va., 19
St. Anne's Church, Annapolis, Md., 23, 44, 48
    Gardiner, Me., 163
    (Appoquinimy) Middletown, Del., 30, 116, 117, 119, 151
St. Barnabas' Church, Leeland, Md., 46, 52, 85
St. Bartholomew's Church, Green Hill, Md., 51
St. David's Church, Cheraw, S.C., 93
    Creswell, N.C., 90, 93
    Radnor, Pa., 117, 119, 126
St. George's Chapel, Indian River Hundred, Del., 119
    Jefferson County, W. Va., 49
    New York, N.Y., 24
St. George's Church, New York, N.Y., 113
    Schenectady, N.Y., 118, 120
    Valley Lee, Md., 51
St. George's Fort, Me., 43, 162
St. Helena's Church, Beaufort, S.C., 93
St. James' Chapel, Elmhurst, N.Y., 120
St. James' Church, Bristol, Pa., 119
    Goose Creek, S.C., 20, 25, 28, 89, 91, 92, 93, 96, 106
    Herring Creek, Md., 47, 52, 80, 81, 90
    Kingsessing, Pa., 119
    Mecklenburg County, Va., 50
    My Lady's Manor, Md., 51
    Perkiomen, Pa., 119
    Santee, S.C., 91, 92, 93

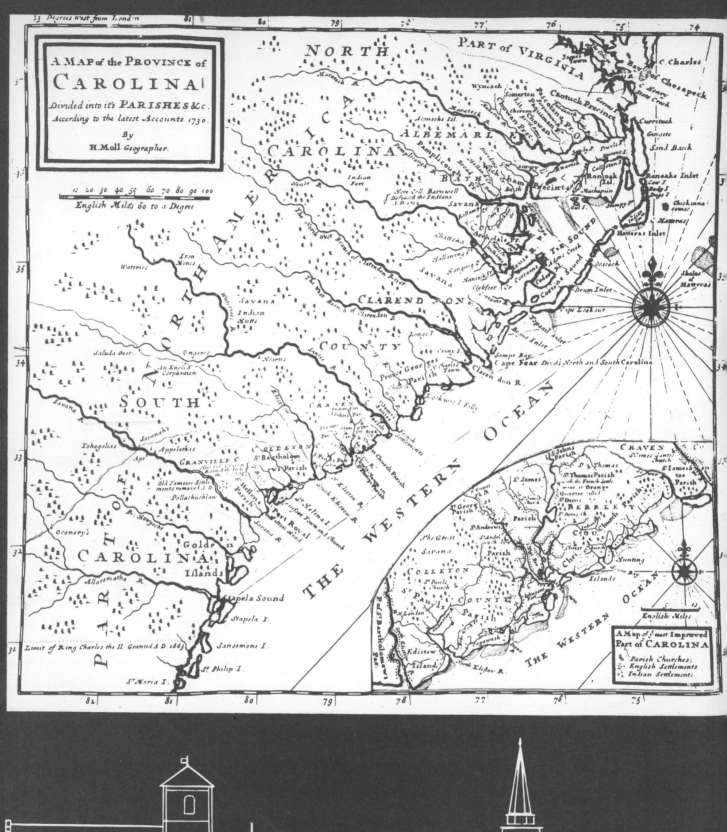

A MAP of the PROVINCE of
CAROLINA
Divided into it's PARISHES &c.
According to the latest Accounts 1730.
By
H. Moll Geographer.

10 20 30 40 50 60 70 80 90 100
English Miles 60 to a Degree

A Map of ye most Improved
Part of CAROLINA

✠ Parish Churches
✠ English Settlements
☐ Indian Settlements

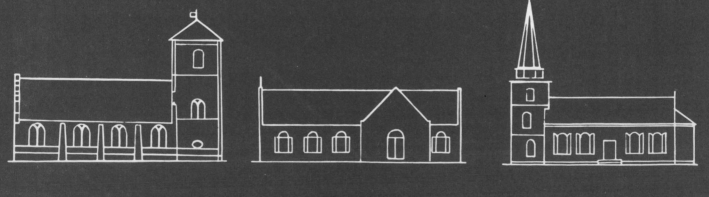